Interpersonal
TECHNOLOGY

The Art and Science of Personal and Professional Effectiveness

JAMES A. GWALTNEY, Ph.D.

Wasteland Press
www.wastelandpress.net
Shelbyville, KY USA

Interpersonal Technology:
The Art and Science of Personal and Professional Effectiveness
by James A. Gwaltney, Ph.D.

First Printing – July 2011
ISBN: 978-1-60047-595-5

Printed in the U.S.A.

0   1   2   3   4   5   6   7   8

Table of Contents

Introduction

Over the years, I have spent thousands of hours in classrooms and seminars, and the intense level of interaction in these settings has provided a rich laboratory for my own learning. Witnessing how people react, viewpoints they reflect, and their amazing blind spots have all contributed to my understanding of human behavior. Over time, this work of observing, teaching, and coaching has been a significant part of the creation of *Interpersonal Technology* (*IT*).

The material in this book is a direct outcome of my working with others to help them develop a greater understanding of human behavior – both their own and that of others. My belief in the value that people derive from exposure to *IT* is my reason for writing this book.

Background

The *IT* perspective is based on both theory and practice. *Interpersonal Technology's* theoretical roots lie in the work of Carl Jung. Its practical base comes from my association with some extremely remarkable people whose personal success has helped me see their strengths translated into successful practice. These individuals have helped me further understand some of the core concepts of *IT* by the way they lived them. I have a deeper understanding of *Interpersonal Technology*, and a stronger belief in its value, having seen the principles operative in the lives of these and other individuals. I will be sharing the stories of eight remarkable people early on in the chapters on key skills.

From the very beginning, it was my goal to develop a system that focuses on day-to-day behaviors in a way that helps each of us gain a deeper perspective on our unique worldview.

The Theory

During my years of service at Southern Methodist University, I also maintained a practice in counseling and psychotherapy. In connection with that part-time practice, I entered into a joint venture of owning office property with Dr. Harville Hendrix and Dr. James Hall. Harville has since become best known as an author and lecturer, and James, despite a debilitating stroke, continues to be recognized as an acknowledged leader in the field of Jungian psychology. These relationships, along with our mutual academic pursuits, spawned my initial interest in Jung.

A very different interest developed, however, through my teaching a course at SMU business school's Institute of Management. The course was variously named over the years, with two of the titles being, "Handling Problem People," and "Mastering the Mystery of Personality." Whatever the name, the experience heightened my desire to help people make practical use of some important interactive insights in their personal and professional settings.

As a result, when I was granted research leave at SMU, I chose to spend my time at the Jung Institute in Zurich. During that time I focused on Jung's work, Psychological Types. I sought to read it from the perspective of making direct application to personal and professional experience. While I found it a marvelous source book for developing insight, I do not recommend it to people who want to understand *Interpersonal Technology*. One reason I do not recommend Psychological Types to people is that it takes a clinical approach. Jung did what you would hope any individual who develops significant insight would do – he put those insights to good use. In Jung's case, being a practicing psychoanalyst meant using his typology to explore possible areas of pathology. Thus, much of the book's focus is on describing where we can go wrong.

Despite its negative tone, Psychological Types nonetheless serves as the foundation of typological psychology. Virtually every system you have ever encountered that describes personality types has its roots in Jung's work. In my case, I was interested in how Jung's insight could provide practical guidelines for understanding behavior in our day-to-day experience. I found that it helped me better explain our behavior in important areas, including how we interact with one another, how we make important decisions, and how we like to get things done.

Concepts can be explained theoretically. I believe, however, they are more powerfully demonstrated by looking at the lives of people who accomplish things that inspire us. Reflecting the truism that "a picture is worth a thousand words," I have provided you a glimpse into the lives of eight remarkable individuals. Through their actions, these eight people paint a picture that adds a special ring of truth to the theories reflected in the *Interpersonal Technology* system.

While no one is successful due to a single dimension of their personality, the success achieved by each of these individuals is connected to a key skill identified within the *IT* system. It was difficult for me to choose between the many individuals who have served as wonderful examples by putting their skills to good use. The ones I have chosen have all achieved remarkable results. They have either headed their own companies or have been in positions of significant responsibility. Each one has been a teacher to me, and I believe they will serve as indirect teachers for you, too.

What You Can Expect

I'd like to make a confession that also serves as a disclaimer. For years, I have been suspicious of people who begin an introduction or start their first chapter by telling you all the incredible benefits you will gain by reading their book. My suspicion is born of having been repeatedly disappointed when the promises don't live up to the expectations they created. As a result, my perspective as a reader is summed up by my own maxim, "The more sweeping the promises, the higher my initial skepticism."

As a consequence of my own promise/doubt ratio, I vowed to myself that this book would not begin with proposed benefits. Nevertheless, as I asked myself how best to entice the reader to become engaged with this material, I could think of no better way than to convey what you can expect from your commitment to understanding *Interpersonal Technology*.

Many years ago, I had the privilege of hearing a gentleman who was on the team that developed the first IBM computer describe his pilgrimage from being an innovator and inventor to an educator and developer of people. One of the things he said that day has remained with me over the years. He said, "A golden rule of learning is the learner must have a sense of clear relevance and felt need." After all these years, I am more convinced of this truth than ever. Thus, I have sought to demonstrate for you, the reader, the relevance and usefulness of the *IT* approach.

What I hope to do is to strike a fair balance between what is exciting and enticing and what is real and factual. John Quigley, Jr., former Vice President of Human Resources for the Dr Pepper-Seven Up Company, often referred to the difference between the steak and the sizzle as the difference between content and excitement. I hope you will find that the *Interpersonal Technology* approach provides you a balanced meal, which includes both significant steak and an appropriate amount of sizzle.

Promises Delivered

One of the things I have learned from working with people in learning settings is that many of the insights they develop are based on their life experiences and their personal perspectives. However, while acknowledging that each reader derives his or her own unique insights from the material, there are some common benefits every reader can expect to gain.

Personal Insight

The fact that you are reading this book suggests that you have an interest in developing a greater sense of personal competence. The degree of effort and experience you have previously invested in developing a higher level of self-awareness will make a difference in the personal insight you receive from the *Interpersonal Technology* system. If you are a relative newcomer to the adventure of self-discovery, you are in for a lot of "ah-ha" moments. If you are a seasoned self-explorer, you are likely to find your rewards in areas beyond initial self-discovery, such as:

- Gaining a new frame of reference for evaluating the behavior of others
- Developing a more systematic means of engaging in interactions
- Discovering new insights about the connection between your behavior and the non-verbal signals you send
- Confirming some of the things you had previously thought about yourself

Whether you are a novice or a pro at self-evaluation, the *Interpersonal Technology* system will give you a realistic profile of yourself. This profile can prevent you from perpetuating the unclear or inaccurate self-perceptions we are all prone to create. One way we blur our self-perception is through making unequal comparisons. For instance, have you ever noticed how we all tend to put a different label on our own behavior than we use to describe the same behavior in someone else? Some of the most commonplace comparisons are:

Self-Perception	Perception of Others
When I Do This I Am:	*When Others Do This They Are:*
Strong Leader	Aggressive & Abrasive
Sensitive	Defensive / Emotional
Firm / Independent	Stubborn / Hard-Headed
Prudent / Economical	Stingy / Tight

The *IT* system will provide you with more objective and accurate perceptions as you describe yourself and others.

Finally, *IT* will also help you see yourself as others see you. We often have a tendency to see ourselves as "just me." By using *Interpersonal Technology* to get a fix on our own tendencies and habitual actions, we can more accurately discover how we appear to others.

Understanding Others

The second major benefit of *Interpersonal Technology* is that you will develop a deeper understanding of others. Having a solid self-understanding and a well-founded basis for understanding others gives us a powerful set of relationship tools.

By using multiple observational tools, *IT* can help you strengthen your powers of observation. By paying attention to expressed preferences, key statements, word choices, and numerous non-verbal cues, you can develop patterns of recognition. This method of understanding is not an innate talent for any of us, but once learned, it will provide you with greater ability to anticipate the behaviors of others.

Sharpening Your Observational Skills

An essential ingredient in being an exceptional leader is the ability to observe and identify what is going on in a given situation. For example, what does a leader need to understand in the brief interchange between two people? The dynamics of the conversation you are about to read could just as easily occur between a husband and wife, or a parent and an adolescent child, as they did between John, the manager of customer service, and Mark, the company comptroller. The dialogue would have been different, but the dynamics the same. The customer service manager begins.

John: "Mark I need to talk with you." (Standing in the doorway)

Mark: "OK, come on in." (Continues to look at his computer screen)

John: "You know I have been working on a new program for customer service." (Speaking with enthusiasm)

Mark: "Yes." (No inflection; still glancing at the computer screen)

John: "Well, I'm ready to talk about approval of funding. I know I'm going to need your support when I go to the executive committee with this. (Spoken with energy and conviction)

Mark: (silence, and non-revealing stare)

John: "Well, what do you think? (Showing some anxiety)

Mark: "I'd need to know a lot more before I can give you my support." (Showing no indication of how he feels)

John: (raising his voice) "Well you certainly didn't ask any questions when I presented this to the committee and got the go ahead!"

Mark: "It didn't sound like you had much information, so I didn't ask." (Showing no reaction)

John: "Well you could have!" (Voice obviously louder and slightly angry)

Mark: "So I'm asking now; how much is it going to cost?" (Direct and firm)

John: "Don't you care anything about how the program works and how it will impact the company?" (Clearly irritated)

Mark: "My job is to know how much it costs, and…." (Interrupted by John)

John: "It doesn't sound like you care at all about our customers and our people." (Strongly emotional)

Mark: "I'd like to see more information and a rational, well thought out proposal." (Showing slight discomfort and withdrawing)

John: "In light of our conversation, I am not feeling very rational right now." (Exhibiting emotion)

Mark: "That's obvious." (Tone indicating disapproval)

John: "I don't know why I thought I could talk to you; I should have known what your reaction would be." (Angry and accusing)

Mark: (silent)

John: (leaves)

It is obvious that a disagreeable exchange has occurred here. It is a lot less obvious why this transaction went off track. It is not at all obvious what the dynamics were, and what strategies could have made this a very different transaction. By the time you complete this book you will understand exactly what was occurring with both parties, and what either one could have done that could have kept the interaction on track. You will know strategies for this situation and for countless others that can improve your interactive effectiveness. You will learn to use non-verbal indicators as a powerful tool for recognizing another person's interactive approach. Moreover, through the use of this distinctive approach, you will learn that exchanges like this are not so much a matter of circumstance as they are of style. Once you learn to detect a person's interactive approach, you will have specific strategies for how to work productively with that person. You will be equipped with the unique tools of *Interpersonal Technology*.

To keep matters in perspective, <u>information</u> technology, the traditional "IT," impacts the way business is conducted at virtually every level. It has brought us everything from sophisticated software systems to the "online" way of life. What it has <u>not</u> done however, is improve the quality of our interpersonal interactions. *Interpersonal Technology* focuses on understanding and improving our interactions with one another. Although the system takes a psychological approach, I refer to it as a technology because it is a logical and systematic approach to self-understanding and to developing strategies for improved interactions. It is truly an art and a science.

It has been personally satisfying over the past thirty years to observe the positive shifts people make after using the principles of *Interpersonal Technology* for a short period of time. This has been especially true for individuals who may have difficulty relating to others. They are naturally skeptical, but overwhelmingly have a positive response after being exposed to *Interpersonal Technology*. I receive comments such as, "This makes sense to me. It gives me a systematic approach for communicating." Others appreciate the fact that they can use the system without having to undergo a personality change.

Interpersonal Technology, the <u>new</u> *IT*, offers a wide range of tools and techniques for improving interpersonal interactions, and does so in a manner that you can understand and quickly master. You will find the information in the remaining chapters can literally help you "read another person like a book." You will be able to identify their style, and to predict key behaviors you can expect of that person in a given situation.

Benefit: Insight versus Magic

There are times when the knowledge gained from *Interpersonal Technology* about another person's likely behavior can appear almost magical to someone unaware of how the system works. The basis for what I describe as the "predictability factor" is mastering the system. (Simply put, the predictability factor is the ability to accurately predict a person's response to a given situation.) No doubt, the idea of magic is exciting to all of us, but in many ways, the insight gleaned through *IT* is far more desirable. Magic implies a happening based on events beyond our control or understanding. Insight, on the other hand, is based on solid knowledge and is available on demand to the person who possesses that insight. Insight allows us to test and exercise the predictability factor consistently. Magic is fun; insight is power!

Whether you are seeking to improve your skills in sales, negotiation, communication, or you just want better quality relationships, you will find that *Interpersonal Technology* provides a valuable set of tools you can leverage to improve your effectiveness.

The following diagram gives you a broad outline of the major parts of the book. For those of you who like the big picture explanation, this will be helpful. If, on the other hand, you prefer a more detailed, step-by-step explanation, be assured that begins immediately after the diagram!

INTERPERSONAL TECHNOLOGY ROADMAP

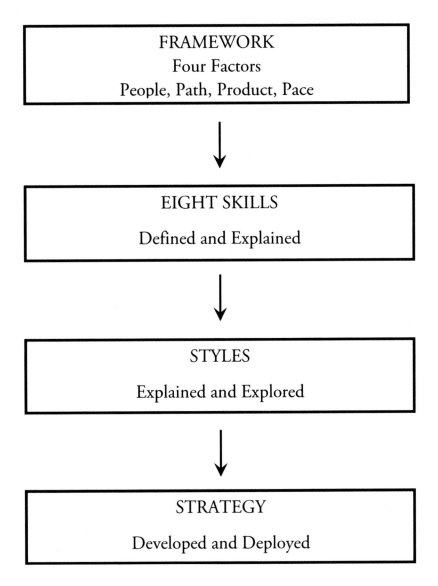

FRAMEWORK
Four Factors
People, Path, Product, Pace

EIGHT SKILLS

Defined and Explained

STYLES

Explained and Explored

STRATEGY

Developed and Deployed

Chapter 1

The Four Primary Categories:
A Structure for Understanding

One of my primary goals is to make *Interpersonal Technology* as clear and direct as possible. One of the ways to ensure clarity is by being systematic. Early in my educational process, I learned the value of using a framework to keep complex issues understandable and manageable.

While most of my high-school friends were still reveling in the glory of graduation, I found myself entering a zoology classroom three days afterward for my first college course.

Besides feeling intimidated about being in class with "adults," the most vivid memory I have is of being a bit overwhelmed with the number of categorizing systems there are in zoology. There was "phylum," the broadest category, and "genus" the more specific, followed by other even more specific descriptions. As bewildering as all this seemed at first, it quickly became apparent that it would be impossible to comprehend all the myriad variety of living creatures without some system of grouping and organizing.

Taking a cue from that early experience, I have provided a framework for understanding the *Interpersonal Technology* system. First, I will present an overview of the general structure, followed later by an exploration of key skills, which ultimately leads to an explanation of our personal styles. We will begin our exploration at the broadest level and move to the more specific, which means we will begin by exploring the basic structure first.

There are four major components that create the structure, or vehicle for helping us understand the primary skills. Each of these are briefly described and explained.

The Four Primary Components

People

The first component, *People*, defines the primary motivation for choosing how we interact with others. This component takes into account our preferences about how we choose to develop relationships, how we are likely to maintain relationships, or how we will terminate them when that is necessary. The *People* factor also helps us understand our preferred manner of handling conflict, and provides insight into our approach when developing personal relationships. It can be described as the "relationship factor."

When we are in a position that requires us to make some assessment of another person's managerial or professional behavior, using *Interpersonal Technology* is a helpful framework for gaining insight about the differing approaches people employ when relating to others.

WHO: The *People* factor describes who we are in regards to our interactive preferences.

Path (Decision Path)

The second category addresses how we make decisions. The *Path* component describes our decision-path.

This refers to our preferred approach for gathering information, processing that information, and arriving at a conclusion or decision. Each of us has distinct preferences for how we make decisions and solve problems, and we often mistakenly assume that everyone goes about the process in the same way we do. Alternatively, when we see that they do not, we may discount their approach as flawed or foolish. One of the things *Interpersonal Technology* helps us do is to understand the differences in peoples' approaches to decision making, and to increase our appreciation of approaches different from our own.

WHAT: The *Path* factor is the point at which we decide what should be done.

Product

Once a decision has been made, that generally requires us to carry through on the decision and produce some meaningful result. Whether in the form of a commitment acted upon, an action taken, or a product produced, it in some way creates an end result. This end result is referred to in the *IT* system as *Product*. It is at the *Product* phase that we actually choose how to get the task accomplished, and go about the business of doing that task.

At times, work groups will have confusion in differentiating the skills connected to the *Path* phase and the *Product* phase. I personally experienced that confusion while living and working in an academic environment for more than a decade. It seemed that oftentimes we would meet to address an issue or problem, we would discuss the issue in great detail, and would decide "in principle" what should be done. A month later, if I asked the embarrassing question of what had been done in regard to our decision, I was often greeted with a chilly silence, or worse yet, a long explanation of the complexity surrounding the issue. What I came to understand was that there was confusion about the difference between making a decision (*Path*) and implementing that decision (*Product*).

At one point, in an act of frustration, I placed a large poster on my office door with a picture of a group of hippos standing in a river, all with their mouths wide open. The caption below the picture read: "When all is said and done around here, more will be said than done." While not very politically correct for the environment in which I was working, it pointed to one of our deficits concerning the *Product* phase.

HOW: The *Product* factor is the point at which we implement our decisions. It begins with addressing <u>how</u> we are going to complete the task.

Pace

Every individual has a preferred *Pace,* or rate of activity, at which he or she works most comfortably. For some, that *Pace* will be quite rapid, while for others it is more reflective. In many ways, this can be seen as the backdrop upon which the other three components operate. Our natural cadence, or preferred tempo, will often be manifested in the other three elements, *People, Path,* and *Product.*

For example, in the *People* area, the *Pace* component will be reflected in how quickly an individual initiates conversation with another person. It may likewise suggest how rapidly one would be inclined to connect with another individual. In the *Path* area, *Pace* will affect speed of the decision-making process. Similarly, when in the *Product* phase, the *Pace* factor will affect how quickly people feel the need to move into implementation.

The simple example may help you get a feel for how pacing influences our behavior. Imagine a host asking you to go into their unfamiliar kitchen and retrieve a corkscrew. Would you go in and immediately start opening drawers, or would you look at the layout and think, "It may be in with the silverware, which is likely to be near the dishwasher," and begin looking there? The answer to which of these is your more likely behavior relates to your preferred *Pace*.

WHEN: *Pace* addresses the rate question. When should we begin?

The Framework

These four primary components provide a framework for understanding the key interactive *Interpersonal Technology* skills. Once you have a thorough understanding of the skills, you will be prepared to comprehend the even more rich and fascinating world of personal styles. Learning about skills will lead to a deeper understanding of your personal style, and will provide you with a frame of reference for understanding others' styles.

As you learn to assess others' skills and styles, these four primary questions can be very helpful:

- How does this person deal with others as they develop and manage relationships?
- How does this person go about reaching conclusions and making decisions?
- How does this person generally complete tasks and act on decisions?
- What is the preferred pace or tempo at which this person works most effectively?

Four Categories: A Blend, Not a Balance

Since we are not born as perfectly balanced beings, it should come as no surprise that we do not have an equal distribution of each of the four categories. You will find in your own experience, as well as through observing others, that one or two of these elements is more pronounced. Not only do we find that individuals have varying degrees of each of the four factors, the same is true for organizations. A dominance of any one of these four components can influence the culture of an organization.

People as the Dominant Component in Organizations (how we make and maintain relationships)

When I think of contexts where the *People* category strongly influences the way organizations express themselves, those that most vividly come to mind are mental health or counseling centers. Having worked in and visited numerous counseling centers, I know that in most cases, maintaining effective relationships is usually a dominant concern. Words such as: openness, transparency, genuineness, trust, respect, and congruence are much more commonplace there than in the average work environment. There is a strong cultural message concerning the importance of relating authentically with others. However, this strong emphasis on the *People* factor may result in a neglect of the *Path* and *Product* factors, leading to organizational dysfunction. The imbalance creates unclear role expectations, organizational vagueness, and inadequate administrative procedures.

Path as the Dominant Component in Organizations (how we gather and process information when making decisions or solving problems)

An experience with a group of engineers at a large engineering company illustrates what happens when *Path* becomes the dominant factor. This particular group had become aware that they were developing a reputation among their peers of "not delivering." They asked for a one-day workshop to analyze some of their work behaviors and determine how to improve their performance.

Among the things I requested they do in preparation was to bring to the meeting a decision of some complexity that the group needed to make, and to be prepared to make it during our session. As they moved through the process of making the decision, we documented the way they went about it.

After almost three hours of work, the group reached a decision and was prepared to look back at the process they had used. In the course of their decision-making, we recorded on newsprint each of the steps they took. Looking around, the newsprint covered three entire walls of a very large conference room. More to the point, however, when they began to review those charts, the group realized that only the last three statements on the very last sheet of newsprint had anything to do with action to be taken. All of the prior steps were analysis. One member of the group said very insightfully, "We are suffering from analysis paralysis."

This situation provides a classic example of what can happen when the *Path* category is such a dominant factor in the culture of a group.

Product as the Dominant Component in Organizations (determining how we are going to complete the task)

Many organizations measure themselves in terms of the commodity they produce, and production becomes the primary focus. Thus, *Product* becomes the dominant factor in shaping the culture. When walking through one manufacturing facility, I saw a banner on the wall with the slogan, "Get it done – Today," which reflected their strong emphasis on *Product*. While this motto can certainly encourage productivity, it also had the unintended consequence of reducing attention to quality issues.

While overusing dominant components carries obvious negative potential, it is important to remember that when managed consciously, it can also produce positive outcomes. Some of the early computer and software companies were examples of consciously creating a culture that would produce the desired product: creative ideas. They did this by providing a climate in which ideas could blossom and grow. Rather than being guided by rigid rules and being highly structured, the emphasis was toward a more free flowing and relaxed environment. This was typified by limitless coffee breaks, and break rooms with ceramic boards designed to encourage creative doodling and sharing ideas. The emphasis on ideas as *Product* reshaped the way organizations looked and behaved. When *Product* is the dominant factor, we are likely to see that acted out in concrete and specific ways.

<u>*Pace* as the Dominant Component in Organizations</u> (the natural cadence at which we work most comfortably)

Pace, the fourth potentially dominant component, is most influential in situations that are particularly time sensitive. A clear example of this type of environment is the activity each business day on the floor of the New York Stock Exchange. However, there are times when this emphasis is due not to industry characteristics, but to leadership preference.

A clear illustration of the influence of a leader's preference is an executive with whom I worked a number of years ago. He was in the construction business. *Pace* was a major driver for the way he worked and managed the business, as typified by a comment he made that I have never forgotten. He said, "I don't care whether I am on the jobsite or in the office. I either want to see dust or paper flying."

In working with his company, it was apparent that everything was constantly in "hurry-up" mode. As you might expect, this was not always driven by circumstance, but more by the executive's personal preference. He simply was not comfortable when things became routine, consistent, or calm. When this was the case, he had the uneasy sense that they were losing momentum. In consequence, he would often create a crisis, as he put it, "just to stir things up." At times, this approach kept the organization ahead of the competition, but at other times it simply met the leader's need for an adrenaline rush.

Pace can influence the manner in which issues are expressed, decisions are made, or action is taken.

Separate but Simultaneous

While it is important to have given you a brief definition of the four factors, it may lead to a misconception. It would be easy to assume that these four fields of activity occur in an orderly sequence, but life is not that simple. It would be nice if you could complete *relating* with people about an upcoming decision, then *make* the decision, and only then address *how* to implement it, but our own experiences contradict that. If, for example, we have a decision that needs to be made, we cannot simply function in the *Path* area and focus only on decision-making. If we do not pay attention to how it affects others and get agreement about our objective, we will quickly be reminded that we do not operate in a vacuum. We must continue to engage and involve others even though the primary goal is to make a good decision. Thus, while the functions are separate in the contribution they make to a positive outcome, they are not as compartmentalized as might be assumed. My shorthand term for this is "*separate* but *simultaneous.*"

IT TV

An example of separate but simultaneous is explained with the analogy of a television screen. The screen is composed of thousands of pixels, each of which contains the four colors of red, blue, green, and black. The signal received by the pixel causes one of the primary colors to light up, and it is surrounded by black. The production of these thousands of tiny lights results in the picture we see on the screen. While the pixels are bound together, each one is called into a dominant role at a key moment in time.

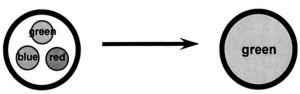

That's what happens to us when we are called upon to focus on one of these areas of activity. One becomes dominant, but it isn't activity taking place in a vacuum. It is occurring while continuing in relationship to the other three.

These four factors represent the structure of *Interpersonal Technology*. If you stop and think about it, whether at work or in our personal lives, there are very few activities we engage in that do not reflect one of these four major areas (People, Path, Product, and Pace). We communicate and relate to others, we make choices and decisions, we implement the objectives we have decided upon, and we influence each of these areas by setting a pace or tempo. Take a moment to think about the day you are about to begin, and think about the activities in which you will engage. Now ask yourself in which of the areas your numerous experiences fit.

- ✓ Which ones come under the area of dealing with people – connecting, communicating, influencing, negotiating, sharing, etc?
- ✓ Which have to do with deciding – choosing a course of action, solving a problem, deciding on a change, etc?
- ✓ Which have to do with how you will accomplish your objectives and decisions, resulting in new approaches, processes, or ways of doing things?
- ✓ And finally, how many times will you establish a pace, set priorities, choose how to spend your time, or set deadlines for yourself or others?

You may identify certain things that you cannot place in one of the four areas of activity, but I suggest it will be very few.

As we move into the skill and style areas, the importance of being aware of these four areas of activity will be evident. For now it is sufficient to give you a sense of the progression of the *Interpersonal Technology* system we are about to explore. We will move from STRUCTURE to SKILL to STYLE to STRATEGY.

INTERPERSONAL TECHNOLOGY ROADMAP

THE EIGHT KEY SKILLS

PEOPLE
how we make & maintain relationships
Skills

Self-Motivated   **Other-Motivated**

PATH
how we gather/process information
Skills

Thinking   **Feeling**

PRODUCT
how we are going to complete task
Skills

Choicing   **Dreaming**

PACE
pace at which we work comfortably
Skills

Active   **Pensive**

PART ONE

From Structure to Skill

With each of the eight skills, I have chosen a person who epitomizes the successful application of the particular skill to produce outstanding results. Each of these individuals is one of eight remarkable people I have had the privilege to work with over my years as a consultant.

The individuals I have chosen exemplify someone who demonstrates a particular skill that has been instrumental in their success. They are each a living example of how to use that skill to become more effective both personally and professionally.

INTERPERSONAL TECHNOLOGY ROADMAP

THE EIGHT KEY SKILLS

SKILLS FOR EACH OF THE FOUR FACTORS
Defined & Described

$$\downarrow$$

The First Skill Set Relates To The

PEOPLE FACTOR

PEOPLE *Factor:* How do I prefer to relate to others, and how do I prefer others to relate to me?

Two Polar Opposite Skills

Self-Motivated $\longleftrightarrow$ Other-Motivated

Chapter 2

INTERPERSONAL TECHNOLOGY

THE FIRST KEY SKILL

"SELF-MOTIVATED"

Defined, Described, Explored

ED MALZAHN

One Of

EIGHT REMARKABLE PEOPLE

Self-Motivated Behavior

Self-Motivation: What motivates us to relate to others in the manner in which we do?

> *Some people are going to like me and some people aren't, so I might as well be me. Then at least, I will know that the people who like me, like me.*
> -Hugh Prather

> *Self confidence is the first requisite to great undertakings.*
> -Samuel Johnson

A Brief Portrait

The story of Ed Malzahn and the success of the Ditch Witch product are in many ways synonymous. More than fifty years ago, this independent-minded thinker invented the first mechanical trencher, thereby freeing laborers from the drudgery of manual ditch digging, and launching an entire series of future products for both above and below ground trenching and boring.

This remarkable company, headed by Mr. Malzahn for over half a century, has continued to be the market leader in developing a wide range of products, and is always on the cutting edge of technology in their field. A large measure of that success is due to his leadership. Having the opportunity to work with Charles Machine Works (the corporate name of Ditch Witch products) over the past sixteen years has allowed me to intimately observe the characteristics of the CEO and the key executives within the company. While there are a number of success factors that have contributed to their accomplishments, the *Self-Motivated* skill with which Ed has led the company has been crucial.

It does not take long to realize that Ed's sense of personal direction comes from within himself. He has a clear set of guiding principles, which he can articulate at a moment's notice. It is equally clear that when a situation arises that calls for a decision about strategic direction for the company, Ed asks himself what he thinks, feels, and believes. It is this internal questioning that becomes the basis for his choices and decisions. Working with various levels within the company has allowed me to see that Ed's clear sense of direction has resulted in the long-term development of a well-defined corporate culture. It is a culture that is well understood and solidly supported throughout the company.

Principles and beliefs are not simply something to be voiced for public consumption; they are strongly held. Unlike some leaders, who may be independent but who lack an internal gyroscope based on core values, Ed's internal value system has been a guiding light for the company. It is one of the major ingredients fundamental to his long-term success.

Another key is Ed's strong sense of technical direction, which he exercises in a self-directed manner. In watching his leadership over the years, it is apparent that he often initiates action through inquiry. Ed frequently walks through the manufacturing or engineering facility and asks a key question of the staff. That question will be pivotal, and oftentimes will redirect the thinking and ultimate direction of a project.

It is clear that Ed understands the power he can exert with a simple question or statement, and consequently, he will often exercise the self-discipline to remain silent in meetings or groups. Even knowing this, there are times when his excitement about an idea or an approach will propel him into speaking out and becoming the dominant force in the meeting.

While he may be impelled to speak in spite of monitoring himself, just the opposite may be true when someone is proposing an idea or concept to him. He is able to refrain from responses and to give few clues about how he is reacting to an idea. You may not know until much later what his judgment on the topic actually was. As a result, people have learned not to go into his office and float trial balloons. Ed's ability to keep his own counsel, coupled with his incisive questions, has taught people that they had better have their facts in order before entering his office for a discussion.

It is these skills and behaviors that have helped form a corporation that enjoys a strong, clear-cut culture with a high degree of alignment. It is a culture that emphasizes sound thinking, and values a practical approach to solving problems.

It is clear that Ed's mature and tactful expression of the *Self-Motivated* skill has been instrumental in the formation of what Ditch Witch has been in the past, and will be in the future.

The Self-Motivated Skill – Defined

When thinking about how we relate to others, there are two primary motivations prompting our interactions. One is sensitive and responsive to the actions and attitudes of others. The second is motivated by one's own internal promptings. People more prone to using *Self-Motivated* skill have a preference for the latter. They are more inclined to express themselves first in interactions, rather than wait for responses and reactions from others. *Self-Motivated* people like to make impact, get reactions, and provoke thought. This skill represents a fundamental orientation in how we choose to relate to others.

A *Self-Motivated* preference holds true whether one is interacting with individuals or groups. The expression of this skill answers the question, "What motivates us to behave in a certain way when relating to others?" Clearly, many factors contribute to our interactive style, but people who are predominately *Self-Motivated* are much more inclined toward self-directed behavior, and operate with a greater degree of independence and autonomy.

This self-directed behavior can take two diametrically opposed forms. First, there is the *Self-Motivated* individual who operates from a position of internal independence. We have all experienced this from someone who says very little, but projects an attitude that makes it very clear they have taken a position, and you will have to prove to them why they should agree with you. It is as if they are constantly saying to you, "Prove it," and you know you are on the spot to do just that! Ed Malzahn is a great example of this.

The second form of *Self-Motivated* behavior is the externally expressive individual. This is the person who will never be overlooked since they are quite willing to speak out forcefully, in groups as well as in individual settings. They take strong positions based upon their own opinions and experience, and are generally not overly concerned about whether others agree with their position.

Whether *Self-Motivated* people express themselves by being more internally independent or more externally independent, they share the common motivation to be self-directed in choosing how they relate to others around them. In some ways, it may not be altogether accurate to describe the behavior as a choice. It is not so much a matter of conscious choice as it is a natural way of being for these individuals. It is their "home base" behavior. It is so natural for them that they may assume other people are only at their best when operating from the same perspective.

The Self-Motivated Skill – Described

A quick way to help you gain an understanding of the *Self-Motivated* skill is through a brief description of some characteristic behaviors associated with its expression. These descriptions highlight some of the most common characteristics.

Need a greater degree of autonomy: Individuals who find it natural to interact through the *Self-Motivated* skill often express discomfort when situations require them to be vulnerable or dependent on others. They like to be the master of their own fate, and report a higher degree of satisfaction when they have a clear sense of being in charge.

More likely to be territorial: *Self-Motivated* individuals will seek to claim and protect physical space as a part of their expression of individuality. A great example comes from my experience in counseling married couples. *Self-Motivated* spouses report the need for more personal space. Oftentimes, the more *Self-Motivated* partner may want a place designated as his or her own and may not want the partner even to enter this sacred space. In work settings, this claiming of space may be physical, having to do with corner offices or larger rooms, or it may be acted out through turf issues.

Major point of reference is within one's self: The *Self-Motivated* individual has a strong sense of internal focus. They will naturally trust their plan, their opinion, and their course of action over those of others. Taking and maintaining a strong position feels natural for these individuals. To persuade *Self-Motivated* people to change their minds and accept someone else's viewpoint requires forceful convincing.

Has a natural tendency to initiate: There are times when the *Self-Motivated* person will initiate activity by giving directions to others. Other times, they initiate by introducing a powerful idea that serves as a catalyst for action. This person often makes things happen, either through direct action or by taking a strong leadership position. The method may vary, but the intent to take initiative is consistent.

Expects others to be comfortable with independent behavior: Their natural independence in relating with others makes it difficult for *Self-Motivated* people to believe that everyone else does not feel the same way. The result is that they find it more difficult to reassure, support, or sustain others, since they do not experience much need for this kind of supportive behavior themselves. I am not suggesting that the *Self-Motivated* person will fail to provide support or express concern for others. I am, however, saying that it will not happen as naturally or come as easily for them as it will for their more *Other-Motivated* counterparts.

Expresses differences of opinion with greater comfort: Due to their own comfort level with verbal or theoretical give and take, *Self-Motivated* individuals will be more direct in their expression of differences. They are also very comfortable with someone who disagrees with them. In fact, they may even feel more at ease with people who will be more argumentative. As one strongly *Self-*

Motivated individual expressed it, "I am more comfortable with someone who will 'mix-it-up' with me; I like to know where people stand."

May be highly reserved or strongly expressive: *Self-Motivation* is not a contrast between shyness and social confidence. People dominant in the *Self-Motivated* skill can represent either of two poles; it is a matter of how the independence is manifested. In some cases, the person will telegraph a clear sense of expectation from others. These individuals assume the other person can read the subtle message of expectation and will react in a way that meets the implied request. This silent expectation is implied rather than explicit.

The other form of *Self-Motivated* behavior is more obvious. It is an outward expression of independence. This may take the form of being more verbally expressive, or of taking independent action. In these cases, there is little doubt in anyone's mind that the person is expressing a form of *Self-Motivated* behavior.

The Self-Motivated Skill – Observed

As is the case with each of the eight skills, there are distinctive non-verbal cues that signal when a person is using a particular skill. The ability to recognize these cues is an extremely valuable asset. In the case of a *Self-Motivated* individual, most of the observable signals represent some element of expressed independence.

The following are some of the most obvious indicators of *Self-Motivated* behavior. As you will see, refusing responsiveness to messages from others takes various forms, but it is often a major indicator of this skill. Response refusal is not a matter of rejection; rather, it is an unconscious expression of independence.

Non-Verbal Indicators

Limiting smile responses: I am not suggesting that strongly *Self-Motivated* people do not smile; nothing could be farther from the truth. They will smile when amused or pleased, and they will often smile to gain a positive response from others. What is different is that they do not feel the *need* to smile in response to a smile-signal sent by someone else. For example, if you arrive at work and greet a *Self-Motivated* person with your best "good morning" smile, they may or may not give you a smile in return. If they are preoccupied or just don't feel their best that day, they will feel no obligation to provide a smile response. You may say to yourself, "What's wrong with them?" The answer may well be: absolutely nothing. They simply feel less need than *Other-Motivated* people to provide social reassurance.

Lack of change in facial expression: We often use a change of facial expression to signal to others that we are listening or are interested in what they have to say. Changing expressions may also be a signal to encourage further comment or to signal agreement. This may take the form of brief smiles, widening of the eyes, or matching the facial expressions of the other person. The *Self-Motivated* person has less need to provide these forms of non-verbal support.

Not nodding the head: People use affirmative nods not only to indicate agreement, but also to indicate support, sustained interest, or to prompt another to continue speaking. Many of us look for these cues as a form of validation. It is not uncommon for *Self-Motivated* individuals to refrain from nodding until they have decided that they agree with you. For highly relational individuals, this lack of responsiveness can be disconcerting. However, it is important to remember that *Self-Motivated* people operate with the assumption that you will take care of yourself and it is not their job to take care of you.

Refusal of eye contact: As with other nonverbal signals, a *Self-Motivated* person's refusal of eye contact is likely a natural behavior, not one employed to punish or attack. This will often take the form of the person continuing to look at something that has captured his or her attention. At work, it may be the computer monitor, or a report they are reading. In any case, they expect you to communicate in spite of their split attention, and they expect you to do so without discomfort.

Adopting an independent posture: Taking an independent posture will happen very early in an interaction. Noticing this behavior can be an extremely valuable clue. It will not only give you information about the person's *Self-Motivated* behavior, it also can be a clue as to what they expect of you.

If you enter a room where a *Self-Motivated* person takes a body position of having the arms folded, you may unconsciously fold your arms to match their posture. (We often do this, by the way, as a means to make non-verbal connection.) If we shift to match their position, *Self-Motivated* people will more than likely change to another posture, such as clasping their hands. It is an unconscious expression of individuality or independence for them to move into a different position. If you then shift to match the new pose, at a sub-conscious level they may question your strength or credibility. This is a case where too much "mirroring" will make you look like a flake! This can be a very important clue in situations where we are seeking to convince, sell, or persuade a *Self-Motivated* individual.

Remaining non-synchronous until experiencing strong agreement with the other party: Here, synchrony describes our non-verbal matching or mirroring the body positions or facial expressions of the other person. Not only will *Self-Motivated* people strike independent postures early in an interaction, they will continue to refuse synchrony until they are in clear agreement with whatever is under discussion.

Providing sustained, unbroken eye contact: In contrast to refusing eye contact, the opposite behavior can also be an indicator of the *Self-Motivated* skill; that is, there are times when they will engage in sustained eye contact. Looking directly into another person's eyes without breaking the gaze is disconcerting to many people. This behavior is expressed by *Self-Motivated* individuals for a number of reasons: to express power, to intimidate, or to exert leadership. In other cases, the *Self-Motivated* person may simply be engrossed in the discussion and is not aware of staring. They may fail to notice your discomfort with their unconscious staring.

The Self-Motivated Skill – Misused

In our culture, many characteristics of the *Self-Motivated* skill are identified with leadership. Many entrepreneurs who make business headlines are dominant in *Self-Motivation*. However, it is important to remember that while every skill holds great potential for good, every skill also has its "shadow" or "dark" side. The following are common instances where this skill can most readily be misused.

Offend without awareness: Sometimes, their presumption that others also operate from a strong *Self-Motivated* position leads them to make statements or take actions that may shock or offend a more relationship-oriented person. In the more extreme of these situations, the *Self-Motivated* person may not even notice the other person's negative reaction.

Risk without prudence: Their strong sense of self-confidence may lead *Self-Motivated* people to overstep the bounds of good judgment at times, and to take risks that do not turn out well. An interesting note about some peoples' misuse of the skill in this manner is that they find it difficult to learn from their mistakes. This is more likely to be the case with a *Self-Motivated* individual who lacks an appropriate level of emotional intelligence. Despite earlier poor results, they seem to maintain a confidence level that makes them a candidate for the next high-risk opportunity that comes their way.

Stifles leadership: Being both independent and self-confident are natural characteristics of the *Self-Motivated* person. This can lead the individual to take on leadership roles quite readily. In many situations, they take the leadership role when it could be important to allow others the chance to take responsibility. As a result, leadership opportunities that could go to others are eliminated.

Disparaging relationship skills: When an individual consistently overuses the *Self-Motivated* skill, it is often because it feels so personally gratifying. This can result in the person so valuing the heady experience of independence and autonomy that they develop a very low opinion of the opposite skill set. When this happens, the *Self-Motivated* person may make disparaging remarks about relationship skills such as empathy or sensitivity to other people's emotional needs. As a result, they may unwittingly cut themselves off from interactions with others who sense the strong bias in favor of self-reliance.

<u>An important reminder:</u>

Having reviewed these potential points of excess, it is important to note that not everyone with the *Self-Motivated* relationship orientation will engage in these behaviors. Most will not, and even those who do so will not engage in the excessive behavior all the time.

A Reflection on Self-Motivated Skill

Just as the Declaration of Independence was a defining event in America's history, we all have defining moments in our own history – our personal declaration of independence. Sometime our declarations are dramatic, or even chaotic. At other times, they may occur so smoothly as to be almost unnoticed. When our declarations do not create upheaval, their import may come only later. In moments of heightened insight, we recognize those incidents that have helped to mold our character, such as:

- Becoming aware of an internal strength that allows us to speak up and speak out.
- Relating to others from a clear-cut, well-defined position.
- Feeling secure enough to disagree in the face of authority.
- Discovering that there are times when silence can be a strong voice.
- Setting boundaries that stop others from intruding.
- Making a choice that fulfills a sense of personal destiny.
- Learning that being strong is more than being aggressive.
- Letting "me be me" and "you be you."

These formative acts originate from the voice within that says, "Listen to yourself. Trust your inner direction. Act on your conviction." When we heed that inner prompting, we know that we are in charge. There is a sense of self-affirmation and self-direction that proclaims, "This is Me!"

Personal Reflection

How clear am I about the defining moment(s) in my life?

Can I identify the resources I draw upon in order to exercise my own *Self-Motivated* skills?

Chapter 3

INTERPERSONAL TECHNOLOGY

THE SECOND KEY SKILL

"OTHER-MOTIVATED"

Defined, Described, Explored

JOHN ALBERS

One Of

EIGHT REMARKABLE PEOPLE

Other-Motivated Behavior

It is well to remember that the entire population of the universe, with one trifling exception, is composed of others.

-James Andrew Holmes

I am a part of all that I have met.

-Alfred, Lord Tennyson

A Brief Portrait

In more than half of my thirty years as a management consultant, one of the highly informative and challenging experiences I was privileged to have was sitting in on the executive staff meetings of the Dr Pepper and later the Dr Pepper/Seven-Up Company. This group of four individuals was in the position of making significant decisions for the corporation at virtually every meeting. Their strong personalities, as well as the differing agendas, made conducting these meetings a demanding challenge. Watching the chairman of the company, John Albers, orchestrate those sessions, and listening to his evaluation of the interactions in the post-meeting debriefing we often had was a continuing learning experience for me.

John's *Other-Motivated* skills allowed him to read the responses and reactions of the participants, to redirect the group when necessary, and to resolve differences with consummate skill. He seemed to possess an innate sense of when to push and when to wait, when to address an issue and when to let it lie.

His ability to read another's agenda was a major guide in deciding how best to involve, include, or to hold at bay an overly aggressive individual. He was able to quickly read agendas ranging from masked motives and self-serving suggestions, to fair and objective assessments, and deeply held corporate commitments. This ability to read, relate, and react, coupled with a genuine acceptance and affirmation of these valuable members of the management team, was a combination that produced ongoing positive results.

While on occasion he would employ the use of a more independent, directive stance, this was certainly much less often than is typical of many people in the position of chairman of a major corporation. John's sparing use of his legitimate power, however, made the occasions he chose to use it much more potent and attention-getting. In contrast with others who often took strong positions or routinely expressed opposition to a new idea, John's selective use of dominance gave it an extra edge.

The strategies and initiatives that resulted from the work of this small but potent team were exceptional. The company's success under John's leadership, centered in his positive use of the *Other-Motivated* skill, is testimony to the value of the judicious use of a key skill.

The Other-Motivated Skill – Described

I have chosen some of the more common characteristics of the *Other-Motivated* skill to share here. While this is not an exhaustive catalog of the attributes I could describe, they are representative of predictable behaviors you will notice.

External in nature: C.G. Jung coined the term "extroversion" as a way of describing individuals more attuned to their environmental and behavioral climates. In relating with others, it is clear that *Other-Motivated* individuals are more motivated by external cues.

Other people as a major reference point: As the term "*Other-Motivated*" indicates, this set of skills places a high value on relationships. A person whose dominant skill preference is *Other-Motivated* generally knows that the dynamics of relationships influence a great deal of what they say and do. This is in contrast to *Self-Motivated* behavior, which places emphasis on self-direction and independence as the major point of reference.

For example, when utilizing *Other-Motivated* skills, we pay careful attention to other people's motives, needs, and opinions, and use them as guideposts for our decisions. I am not suggesting that a person expressing *Other-Motivated* skills is without opinion or direction of their own. Rather, I am suggesting that they are keenly attuned to the opinions and needs of others, and take those into consideration as part of their own decision-making process. One seminar participant who is strongly *Other-Motivated* expressed this well when she said, "It is not that my opinions are not ultimately based upon my own values and beliefs. It's just very important to me that I hear and understand the thoughts, feelings, and beliefs of other people. I use this input to weigh my own choices and decisions. Some people may see this as wishy-washy; I see it as a very important component to making well-informed choices."

Reading signals in others as a valuable asset: In many ways, it appears that people who are strongly *Other-Motivated* have "invisible antennae" that pick up subtle signals much more effectively than is the case with *Self-Motivated* behavior. Someone operating from an *Other-Motivated* skill set will naturally notice both verbal and non-verbal signals from individuals and from groups.

As one person in the mental health field expressed it, "I don't think about reading signals, it's such a natural part of how I interact. I assess situations automatically. It just feels natural to me. And usually, I don't realize that I have done anything differently than others until I make a comment about my observations, and find other people completely surprised about what I have noticed."

A relationship builder: There is a natural drive toward affiliation or making connection. Making positive connections feels important to the *Other-Motivated* individual, and consequently, they will work harder to develop and maintain positive relationships.

Encourages flexibility: *Other-Motivated* individuals want to be as open as possible to the ideas of others, so they are more likely to find that point of contact, that area of agreement, which will generate practical solutions while at the same time developing a relationship. The behavioral outcome is greater flexibility in their dealings with others.

More motivational than directive: The *Other-Motivated* skill set is more likely to take into account the wants and needs of others. As a result, they resort to motivational techniques keyed to their understanding of what drives or inspires the other person. They will be much less inclined to ignore or discount the needs and values of others when in a leadership position.

Enjoys collaborative projects and initiatives: One of the quickest ways to lose the contribution of an *Other-Motivated* individual is to place them in an isolated work environment for a long period of time. As one strongly *Other-Motivated* individual expressed to me, "If my manager puts me in a closet, so to speak, and allows me no contact with others, I lose my energy and enthusiasm very quickly. And, it won't be long before I'm looking for another job."

Non-Verbal Indicators

The non-verbal clues that indicate *Other-Motivated* behavior are fueled by the need to develop positive relationships. As a result, the non-verbal behaviors are often prompted by an unconscious motive to make connection, or the need to maintain a relationship. This natural maintenance behavior can be observed in non-verbal signals that help the other party feel comfortable. The behaviors primarily observed and described in this section revolve around high response behavior, communication connectors, and synchrony.

Highly responsive behaviors: If you greet an *Other-Motivated* person with a smile, they will generally respond with a smile of their own. They react in response to the other person. For example, if their counterpart leans forward, the *Other-Motivated* person will lean forward as well. Similarly, if the other person lowers their voice, an *Other-Motivated* person will also lower their voice level. These responsive behaviors are intended to create comfort.

Communication connectors: *Other-Motivated* people will incorporate a number of responses designed to encourage contact and increase positive communication. These responses include changing their facial expression to reflect agreement or acknowledgment, nodding the head, widening the eyes, smiling, or other prompters to indicate that the other person is being heard.

An interesting note on this behavior: Many public speakers have reported to me that they have to be on guard against becoming "trapped" by an audience member who exhibits a number of these communication connectors. They create great comfort for the speaker and are extremely responsive. If not careful, the speaker will focus on that person to the exclusion of others in the audience. During my years of coaching people who were preparing for a presentation, this pitfall became so common that I developed a term for the phenomenon: "the friendly face syndrome."

Synchrony: The *Other-Motivated* person will adopt similar postures and body positions as a means of indicating affiliation. This may include changing the way one is sitting, or other unconscious matching behaviors. Synchrony becomes particularly apparent when there is a group of people who are all *Other-Motivated.* I often demonstrate the presence of synchrony by asking a group to freeze their behavior and pointing out the number of matching body positions in the room. The common response is surprise, because their synchronous behavior is so natural they are unaware of it.

The unifying factor in all these indicators is that they are designed to create relationship and enhance positive communication. As a result, it may be more difficult for you to read the non-verbal signals of *Other-Motivated* individuals since they will quickly create non-verbal positions similar to yours. Their particularly quick and unconscious move into synchrony will make reading non-verbal cues more challenging.

The Other-Motivated Skill – Misused

As I pointed out about the *Self-Motivated* skill, there are situations in which we can misuse each of the eight skill sets. In this section, we will explore several ways we can misuse the *Other-Motivated* skill.

Since much of the behavior related to the *Other-Motivated* skill centers around developing and maintaining positive relationships, a number of the potential misuses of this skill relate to an overemphasis on affiliation behavior. The following are some of the most common.

Unintentional impressions of agreement: The tendency to nod positively while listening is a major reason for misconstrued agreement. For the *Other-Motivated* person, nodding the head often means simply, "I am listening; I am tuned in to what you are saying." It does not necessarily mean they agree. If you are communicating with an *Other-Motivated* person, you may be surprised to discover later that the person, in fact, did not agree with you at all, but was simply being responsive.

This *impression of agreement* can also been seen in organizational behavior. In meetings where issues are skirted to maintain harmony, people often leave the meeting assuming support for their position. This can cause significant miscommunication and trust issues in the long run.

The *impression of agreement* is also a standard ploy on many family sitcoms. For example, when the hapless husband leaves alternating messages to his wife and then to his mother, they both think they have his agreement. In sitcoms, it can be an amusing dilemma. However, in real life it can also be quite prevalent, and it is not so funny.

May be overly flexible when hammering out agreements: When this skill is misused, there may be a tendency to "give away" too much when negotiating an issue. This is often prompted by the belief that being flexible and offering concessions will result in the development of trust and cooperation. Sadly, it often backfires. Rather than increasing trust and cooperation, it often has the effect of raising the other party's level of expectation, resulting in their demanding more and expecting even greater flexibility. This response can be bewildering for the *Other-Motivated* person, who feels they have acted in good faith and reached out to the other party.

Tendency to delay task and build relationship: The strong relationship orientation of the *Other-Motivated* person can result in a lack of balance between maintaining relationships and focusing on necessary tasks. For example, an *Other-Motivated* person will be inclined to spend significant time in rapport building when meeting with a new individual. To the more *Other-Motivated* person, this feels comfortable. Meanwhile, a more *Self-Motivated* person may feel like an inordinate amount of time is being spent on the personal side of the equation when there may be pressing work issues at hand.

This extreme focus on the people side of the equation can also result in lower productivity in the work environment. While there is certainly nothing wrong with building rapport or exploring relationships, it is a matter of balance. Strongly *Other-Motivated* people need to be aware of their tendency to overemphasize relationships, and keep in mind the need to balance this behavior with a focus on the tasks to be accomplished.

Failure to express one's opinion in the presence of apparent opposition: Not only does this sometimes leave the impression of agreement mentioned earlier, it also deprives others of input. Withholding an opinion also occurs in the context of speaking up in large groups. Part of this tendency not to speak up is based on the desire to avoid creating conflict. Expressing our opinion when we do not know the various opinions of others in the group may feel like high-risk behavior. For the *Other-Motivated* person, the result is a strong temptation to "self-censor" and rob the world of their input.

Inappropriate sharing of sensitive information: This misuse of the *Other-Motivated* skill often occurs when sharing takes on a more personal nature. The more *Other-Motivated* person may share information – again, to create affiliation – that feels overly personal to the other party. When this happens, the other person may unconsciously withdraw, leading the *Other-Motivated* person to seek connection by becoming even more personal. In this dynamic, the unacknowledged *approach-withdrawal-approach* dance leaves both parties feeling awkward.

Tendency to characterize Self-Motivated behavior as callous or uncaring: Sometimes individuals are so locked into one side of the skill pendulum they come to view the converse skill as negative, especially if they are uncomfortable exercising that counterpoint skill. This tendency can often be observed in group behavior, when the group is heavily weighted toward one side of the skill pendulum. They may build a collective perception that reinforces the goodness and value of their skill preference, and view the opposite skill set as somewhat negative.

Tendency to confuse work relationships and personal relationships: Since it is more natural for *Other-Motivated* individuals to enjoy developing and maintaining personal relationships, they may expect colleagues to respond in ways more appropriate for friendships rather than work relationships. When others do not react in the same way, the person misusing the *Other-Motivated* skill will likely feel betrayed and disillusioned.

Failure to set clear boundaries: In healthy relationships, we know how to set limits and give others clear signals about what those limits are. When we misuse the *Other-Motivated* skill, however, we may not set those limits. The result is that we may allow others to take unfair advantage of us, leaving us feeling resentful while we continue to ignore setting appropriate boundaries.

Tendency to withdraw rather than address situations directly: This is a misuse of the *Other-Motivated* skill when it would be much more productive to engage the other party directly to discuss and settle issues. The rationale for not being direct is based upon fear that we may damage the relationship. The obvious result of choosing non-action is to develop a relationship that is vague and has many unresolved issues. Moreover, rather than improving the relationship, this behavior often results in a feeling of general unease and strain that is counterproductive.

A Reflection on the Other-Motivated Skill

Who we are at any point in our lives is a riddle solved by an inventory of our time and attention, which changes with time and circumstance. One of the keys to the riddle lies in our relationships with others. How we are relating with others can tell us a great deal about who we are at any point in our lives.

When we view ourselves through the prism of our relationships, we are afforded a glimpse of what we value and how we are living out those values. The act of making connection can also be a source of pleasure and a means of personal growth. It is an enhancement of our being when we:

- Develop a level of caring deep enough for others to sense and receive our caring.
- Listen to others in a manner that lets them feel respected and appreciated.
- Build bonds of trust by being trustworthy.
- Help someone feel special and important.
- Talk about things just for the pleasure of sharing.
- Let others know we understand on more than a superficial level.
- Appreciate a person based more on character and stature than on status and prestige.

These and other acts of connection help us define who we are. Our interactions provide a mirror that reflects who we are. We are reminded by how we live our lives – how we work, play, share, and love. Unlike our ego, the mirror never lies. It is only a question of how intently we look.

Personal Reflection

How willing am I to examine the quality of my relationships?

When I consider the nature of my relationships, how clearly do my actual relationships match my espoused values?

Are there elements of the *Other-Motivated* skill I would like to alter? If so, what?

INTERPERSONAL TECHNOLOGY ROADMAP

THE EIGHT KEY SKILLS

```
┌─────────────────────────────────────────────┐
│   SKILLS FOR EACH OF THE FOUR FACTORS         │
│            Defined & Described                │
└─────────────────────────────────────────────┘
                      │
                      ▼
┌─────────────────────────────────────────────┐
│        The Second Skill Set Relates To The    │
│                PATH FACTOR                     │
└─────────────────────────────────────────────┘
```

PATH *Factor:* How do we go about gathering and processing information in order to make a decision or solve a problem?

Two Polar Opposite Skills

Thinking ⟵─────────⟶ Feeling

Chapter 4

INTERPERSONAL TECHNOLOGY

THE THIRD KEY SKILL

"THINKING"

Defined, Described, Explored

JOHN HOTZ

One Of

EIGHT REMARKABLE PEOPLE

Thinking Skill

All men by nature desire to know.

-Aristotle

The sign of an intelligent people is their ability control emotions by the application of reason.

-Marya Mannes

You may derive thoughts from others; your way of thinking, the mould in which your thoughts are cast, must be your own.

-Charles Lamb, <u>Essays of Elia</u>, 1823

A Brief Portrait

I first met John Hotz in a team building session at Lakeway, a well-known retreat center in Austin, Texas. I entered the room knowing only the general manager of the six division heads of the Hydril Corporation. As John introduced himself, I felt a subtle degree of reserve that signaled I was going to have to prove myself and the value of this teambuilding effort. His demeanor was not judgmental or resistant; however, it sent the message that performance was expected and that my input would be carefully measured for relevance, soundness, and usefulness. In the nicest of ways, I knew I had been put on notice!

During the early part of the session, while I presented the concept and approach I was suggesting we use for the next two days, John listened intently, but his facial expression gave no indication as to how he was receiving the information. As the process unfolded and he began to get a mental picture of what I was suggesting, he became increasingly responsive.

As he began to make comments to the team, it was apparent that John had the ability to think with greater depth and breadth than his colleagues. His comments early on served the purpose of summarizing the present situation and suggesting implications for the future. Without any formal acknowledgment, it was clear that John filled the role of informal leader, setting the tone and direction for the team.

During the next two days, John would remain silent for relatively long periods, and then at key points he would provide information about how the focus of discussion related to current work issues. Other times he would point out how the discussion raised operational or philosophical issues for the group. Each time he raised points for consideration, he would describe the situation, explain the basis of his judgment, and propose a desired response or course of action.

When John chose to speak to the group, he often did so for several minutes, but the group showed no impatience or the loss of attention frequently seen when one member speaks for prolonged periods. It was clear that at some level the team understood the important role he was fulfilling.

Over the next two days, it became apparent to me that while John had a considerable number of skills that accounted for his managerial success, the cornerstone of that success was his skill as a sound thinker. His ability to see the facts, to assemble those facts into a meaningful whole, and to insist that once brought to light they not be ignored, made him a very effective leader.

When I later had further opportunity to work with John and his management team, I saw the same analytical process. His ability to build fact upon fact in a compelling manner and to set forth the charter and challenge for his own work group was a hallmark of his leadership approach. As I observed this behavior over time, it became clear that John's belief in the power of factual information was a core philosophy.

This philosophy also reinforced a behavior that allowed him to make things happen in his organization. The elusive "success behavior" for John lay in his ability to say very direct and challenging things with a kind of factual neutrality that was very disarming. It was as if he gained added permission to say things that would otherwise be perceived as threatening or challenging because he communicated with the matter-of-fact attitude, "Hey, I'm only saying what's obvious."

I believe it is more than just the skillful use of information that made John an effective leader. There are many people with strong analytical ability who do not achieve leadership effectiveness. The factor that set John apart from many other talented thinkers was his philosophy that the truth is to be sought as the basis for action, not for intellectual superiority.

This belief that the truth, once discovered, cannot be ignored and needs to be acted upon also produced a leadership style very different from the charismatic and emotion-centered style of many visible leaders. In contrast, his style helped others to understand the philosophy: "Seek the truth and the truth shall spur you to action."

The Thinking Skill – Described

The word, "thinking," is used in so many contexts that it is important to be more specific about its definition here. As has been indicated, the *Interpersonal Technology* system was based upon the work of Carl Jung. In his <u>Psychological Types</u>, Jung provides a somewhat narrow definition. After a period of careful observation, Jung chose the word, "thinking" as a descriptor for a certain segment of people within the population who were consistently more logical and analytical in their approach to processing information and making decisions, described as "thinking over feeling."

In the *IT* approach, the *Thinking* skill centers for the most part on the decision making process. How an individual responds to the necessity for a decision, and the manner in which he or she seeks to solve problems, are examples of the use of this skill. For the most part, the process concerns how an individual receives information, organizes data, and reaches conclusions about the assembled facts.

In many ways, the *Thinking* skill is related to what has traditionally been described as the "rational" approach to decision making. There is a strong emphasis on analysis and logic. Characteristics that may be helpful in identifying when a person is using the *Thinking* skill as a preferred behavior are as follows:

A clear need for data: If the person dominant in *Thinking* skill is required to make a decision, insistence on adequate information will be a hallmark of the process. If the person does not believe there is adequate information, he or she will often refuse to go further without the necessary data. Even when others are trying to assure them of the validity of an approach, those with dominant *Thinking* skill will be very uncomfortable if they believe they are being asked to decide without first-hand information. If this person is in a position of power, others will quickly learn that asking for a decision without providing abundant information to back up a proposed action will usually result in refusal.

Preference for written information: Since the *Thinking* skill dominant person seeks to put information into a logical order and to understand how the information relates to present realities, having information that can be referred to more than once will be important. For that reason, oral information is viewed as less useful and is less valued.

The amount of written information this type person desires will depend upon a combination of the other skills we will be reviewing. Some individuals who are strongly oriented toward the *Thinking* skill will want fuller written accounts. Others will prefer the information in outline or bullet form.

Nevertheless, virtually all *Thinking* skilled individuals will express appreciation for information presented in a form that can be referenced on an ongoing basis.

Preference for linear logic: Putting things in a logical order is a natural part of moving through the decision making process for the *Thinking* type. If you ask these individuals how they arrived at a conclusion, they will generally take you through a step-by-step process. If you ask them three weeks later, you will get exactly the same explanation. Moving through the A-B-C's of information leads *Thinking* persons to a decision they are more likely to trust.

A need to deliberate: Because it takes longer to move through a logical step-by-step process, it is important for *Thinking* types to have sufficient time to check each point or fact and make certain it fits with all the others. Even after having taken the time to move through a logical path, *Thinking* skill dominant people will often want additional time to reconsider the facts. For this reason, building in time for deliberation is an important element in their behavior. Others' refusal to allow for that time can result in stalling or stonewalling by this person in order to gain the time they need to make a sound decision.

Willingness to check the facts: While others might be tempted to assume the facts are there to back up a claim or a contract, the *Thinking* skill person will pursue the details to assure that those facts and claims are justified. In this regard, the use of this analytical approach can be of great value in organizational environments.

Non-Verbal Behavior – The Thinking Skill

We know from neuro-linguistic programming (NLP) that certain behaviors are cues to an individual's brain processes. That is nowhere more evident than in the non-verbal indicators of the *Thinking* skill.

When considering non-verbal cues that indicate *Thinking* activity, it can be helpful to keep in mind the work of Sperry and Ornstein on left-brain and right-brain behavior. As most people are aware, left-brain behavior is strongly related to the more linear and analytical approaches.

In observing individuals who are engaged in this more left-brain or *Thinking* function, it is clear that a major non-verbal characteristic is *physical stillness.* It appears that external activity interrupts the more internal and structured reasoning process. As you will see below, you will be able to recognize when someone is engaging in the *Thinking* function by observing their restricted movement.

Non-Verbal Indicators

Limited use of hands and arms: An obvious way to create stillness around us is to limit movement of the hands, feet, and arms. When we are using the *Thinking* skill set, we may sit with hands folded as a way to limit movement. This may also include making gestures that do not exceed the width of the body. It can be described as gesturing from the elbows in.

Arms crossed to ensure limited movement: Despite popular myth, crossed arms do not always means someone is feeling resistant or that they are cold! More often, we fold our arms when we are listening intently and analyzing the information we are receiving. A classic pose of instructors or professors when listening to a question from a student is to face the student with arms folded and little show of emotion. It is not a position of resistance, but one of internal analysis.

Lack of change in facial expression: Not only do we limit movement of the hand, feet, and arms, we limit movement of muscles in the face, sometimes called a "flat affect." This lack of expression often leaves others guessing about what is going on with the person. It would be helpful if the person in the *Thinking* mode were more aware of this and would occasionally give a brief reassuring smile. However, doing so would tend to break their cycle of internal analysis and is not likely to happen.

Tendency to desire more distance, often indicated by slightly more reserve when interacting with others: As with limiting movement, increasing space is a means of reducing the external stimuli. An example of this we can all relate to is doing mathematics. Mathematics is about as pure an example of the more left-brain, *Thinking* skill that we experience. We can all imagine what it would be like for someone to walk up and begin moving things around on our desk while we were calculating a math problem. It would create a sense of irritation, since their behavior would break our sequence of logical thinking. More so than others, the *Thinking* skill dominant person prefers more distance when analyzing or evaluating an issue.

Lack of eye scanning: Too much scanning stimulates the right side of the brain and encourages more *Feeling* skill behavior. This is why people will often fix their gaze on a specific spot on the floor or ceiling when being analytical. Making eye contact adds more stimuli, which we attempt to limit during periods of logical thinking. This is especially true for *Thinking* dominant individuals.

Irritation signaled when other are moving objects or moving themselves in too close proximity: As noted above, for *Thinking* skill people it is particularly irritating to have someone begin to move things on the desk or to move into their personal space when they are engaged in logical analysis. One of their non-verbal responses is a facial expression of irritation designed to suggest that the other person back off! The offending party often misinterprets this disapproval signal as personal, rather than as a need for space and stillness.

Longer than average periods of silence before responding to a question that requires analysis: It takes a bit longer to move through the logic process and formulate an answer than it does to give a spontaneous response. Because of this, there is sometimes a moment of silence before responding that is longer than others may require.

The Thinking Skill – Misused

As with each of the skills, our greatest misuse of the *Thinking* skill is the result of over dependency on or inappropriate expression of the skill. This is generally due to the desire to stay in our own comfort zone. The result is that we fall back on patterns of behavior that are more comfortable to us, even when they are counterproductive. The following misuses of the *Thinking* skill may serve as a checkpoint for you about your use or misuse of this particular skill.

Drowning others in data: Because people dominant in *Thinking* skill view data as a vital ingredient in decision-making and problem solving, they tend to assume that others have a similar preference. As a result, they may give the other party more information than is helpful. This becomes particularly critical in the case of selling or persuading, where such behavior may "turn off" the other person. Oftentimes, the individual who is inundating the other person with information is so personally involved in what they are sharing that they do not notice they have lost the other person's interest.

Tendency to gather information far beyond the point where it is productive: An overuse of the *Thinking* skill sometimes results in a level of perfectionism about being correct that is counterproductive. In this instance, it has to do with timing. When they insist on getting more data even when confronted with the need to make an important decision <u>now</u>, their effectiveness is seriously in question.

This matter of timing is often a point of contention in marriage and family interactions. When one family member is eager to make decisions within a certain time frame and the other partner constantly insists they need more data, conflicts often flare.

Desire to use logic in situations that clearly require an intuitive approach: There are clearly situations that require the use of logic. Reading a balance sheet or balancing one's checkbook would be examples of situations where using the *Thinking* skill is the obvious choice. But when you are dealing with a complex interpersonal situation involving several conflicting personalities, it does not make sense to try to sum up the situation in some sort of formula. In those cases, we need to be able to consider all the various nuances and subtleties even though they do not fit into a neat, logical package. A problem arises for the *Thinking* skilled person when their desire for logic overrides their willingness to approach an issue in a different way.

Tendency to judge the Feeling skill (polar opposite) in an extremely negative light: Describing their interactions with *Thinking* types, *Feeling* skill people, who make decisions in a more global and intuitive manner, often report that they are viewed by their counterparts as a bit "out of control" or "irrational." In many cases, the *Thinking* skilled person is unable to see the validity of an idea when the method for developing that concept does not appear to be logic-based. This discomfort with more intuitive or emotional decision making can lead the *Thinking* type person to withdraw from interacting with the *Feeling* type due to his or her own uneasiness with an alternate process.

Penchant for prudence: Some people have what is commonly referred to as a penchant for risk. Individuals with predominance in the *Thinking* skill are more inclined to have a penchant for prudence. While this may be a good thing in moderation, it becomes problematic when carried to extremes. Being overcautious about the potential for error robs the individual of the courage to risk.

Internal cynicism or voicing cynicism about highly positive personalities: Since the *Thinking* skill process encourages weighing one fact in contrast to another, there is a tendency to withhold judgment until careful consideration is complete. The *Thinking* skill encourages moderating one's emotional reactions for fear they could cloud judgment. It is a short step from this fear to mistakenly assuming that people who are highly positive and enthusiastic run the risk of being in error. There is often an underlying assumption that to be highly effective we need to be moderate in our behavior. When an individual is highly positive or enthusiastic, they may be perceived as being foolhardy.

Failure to engage others at an emotional level: It is common for us to want to remain in our own comfort zone; however, it may not always be productive. In the case of the *Thinking* skill, this comfort zone includes logical and analytical reasoning. Refusal to move beyond that zone can result in a failure to connect with others at a significant emotional level.

Tendency to view every situation as one that can be distilled into a logical equation: Having a world that is logically tidy, having everything make reasonable sense, is a deep-seated desire of the *Thinking* skill. This desire can result in a misuse of the skill, however, when we attempt to turn complex interpersonal situations into mathematical equations. To do so suggests that we need to oversimplify the subtle factors in an attempt to explain tremendously complex realities.

Insisting on more detail than is necessary: Attention to detail is a saving grace in many situations, but it becomes a misuse of the *Thinking* skill when we insist on detail in order to give ourselves a sense of personal assurance.

Ignoring emotional issues and thereby screening out important input: An obvious way we can maintain our comfort level in the *Thinking* skill mode is to ignore or deny behavior. Much of the time, this occurs when the issues are emotional.

Stifling intuitive hunches that can provide important information: All of us are blessed with intuitive ability. Nonetheless, that gift can be sorely underutilized through misuse of the *Thinking* skill. When we have an intuitive flash but immediately discount its validity, we often lose important information.

Reflection on the Thinking Skill

Some years ago, IBM produced a poster to emphasize their technological prowess that consisted of one word in capital letters: THINK. A friend of mine, Daryl Vines, who was then an engineer at Texas Instruments and went on to join the engineering faculty at Texas Tech University, had a phrase he coined that had a similar notion: "Don't just do something, think!" Both of these statements reflect the influence rational processes have had on our technological progress. In reaction to this emphasis, some camps have disparaged analytical thinking as cold and impersonal.

When we engage in these kinds of put-downs, we overlook the pleasure of addressing a mental challenge. Whether as simple as solving a crossword puzzle or as complex as unlocking the genetic code, there is pleasure derived in the effort. To relegate analytical thinking to mere mechanical activity is to deny the life of the mind.

All of us have experienced a moment of internal pleasure when our attempts at logic have fallen into place. In that moment, the process moves beyond the rational to the deeply personal.

- It is a time when we see the poetry in precision.
- It is the reassuring, unbroken line of logic.
- It is the balance and symmetry when facts fit.
- It is the black-white, yes-no reality.

- It is the satisfaction of proper sequence.
- It is the consistent path we can travel again and again.
- It is the inevitable result at the end of a sound process.

This sense of logic gives order and meaning in a world that often feels chaotic and random. Far from mere cold facts and data, logic is a companion that offers a sense of satisfying certainty.

Think about it.

Chapter 5

THE FOURTH KEY SKILL

"FEELING"

Defined, Described, Explored

BOB ZINCKE

One of

EIGHT REMARKABLE PEOPLE

The Feeling Skill

*Epiphanies are unexpected insights born out of the message of the
moment and the accumulated wisdom of our life experiences.*

-James A. Gwaltney, Ph.D.

A Brief Portrait

I asked Bob Zincke to send me a brief biography page to use as a part of his
introduction to six other CEOs who had agreed to spend a day in a roundtable
discussion. His response was brief indeed. He wrote:

> I graduated from Ohio University
> Worked for Kroger for 41 years
> Retired as Executive Vice-President, Corporate

However, far more transpired in the process of making this simple, three-line
bio a reality.

It began with his first boyhood job, when he bought baby chicks and sold
them door-to-door during the Easter season. He quickly learned that he was
dealing with a perishable product, and changed from his live bird business to
door-to-door sales of gift-wrapping accessories. At an age when most boys were
pursuing more playful pastimes, Bob was learning his first lesson in successful
business.

What makes for success is rarely as simple as one way of behaving or a
single stroke of luck. Still, in most situations one or two factors are clearly
instrumental. In Bob Zincke's case, the most influential factor was his wise and
skillful use of the *Feeling* skill. His ability to use situations as learning tools and
to draw upon that knowledge base as the foundation for future decisions is
evident throughout his career.

Bob's ability to get ahead of the learning curve was apparent when he
reported for work at Kroger three days after graduation from Ohio University.
His first assignment was to spend a year in a management training program. In
those days, the program consisted of being assigned to various departments
over the course of a year, with no formal learning structure.

In listening to Bob describe the training experience, it became clear to me
that, while there were no formal sessions for consolidating his learning, he was
learning nonetheless. It was equally clear that he was using the *Feeling* skill to

do so. As he put it, "I learned by osmosis." Learning by osmosis implies sensing situations and combining them in a manner that builds an experience base, which itself becomes a resource for future decisions.

Describing the consolidated experience he gained from that "training program," Bob said, "I saw a lot of things we were doing wrong, and I made a basic decision that became a rule for the rest of my career. That decision was that I would treat people with respect and trust them to do their jobs." Bob's second bedrock decision, also borne out of experience, was that listening to people provides the basis for sound business decisions. These two *"osmosis factor"* conclusions became the operating principles that formed the cornerstone for his leadership approach.

When Bob came to Houston in 1986, he faced a challenge that called for extensive use of his management principles. First, there was the obvious fact that the union contract they had at the time made Kroger's cost of doing business significantly higher than the competition. Opening communication with the employees, and then listening to their views, ultimately led to the restructuring of the contract, and was a first step in Kroger becoming competitive. The second step was a major event for Kroger in Houston and beyond.

In 1992, Kroger Houston was in the unenviable position of having 17.1% of the market share while its major competitor had a 27.6% market share. To address this crisis, Bob, along with a host of employees, developed the concept of the *Signature Store*. Again, listening and also sensing the implications of what they heard produced a resounding success. A task force of employees at all levels of the organization shared their views of what was needed to make the best environment, the best shopping experience, the best possible grocery. Decisions from this several-month process led to a new exciting concept. The *osmosis factor* was alive and well.

The final component included learning from the customer. Seventeen thousand letters were sent to customers asking what they wanted in an ideal grocery. They received an astounding 2000 responses with customers' ideas and expectations, and ninety percent of the suggestions were incorporated into the new concept. The outcome was the birth of the *Signature Store*.

Learning by listening, and making the required decisions based on the messages from employees and customers, produced a dramatic competitive shift. By 1998, Kroger enjoyed a 29.5% market share, and their former chief competitor had 19.68%.

The ability to make the best use of the *Feeling* skill not only meant that Bob learned and made intuitive decisions that paid off. It also meant that employees and customers alike could sense that he not only thought this was the right thing, he *felt* it to be the right thing. The sense of conviction that accompanied Bob's *Feeling*-based decisions was a major component in his leadership successes.

In some ways, you might crystallize this element of Bob's leadership style with the series of words: look, listen, learn, leap – but this is not a blind leap. It's an informed leap, infused with his faith in the wisdom and the capability of both customers and employees.

Bob's ability to make the mental leap from an immediate situation to a conclusion validated by his personal experience has helped him stay a step ahead of the competition. His use of the *Feeling* skill described in this chapter has made Bob a *signature person* in the truest sense of the word.

The Feeling Skill – Defined

As was the case with *Thinking* skill, the *Feeling* skill centers on the decision making process. We will consider what goes on when we make a decision using the *Feeling* skill. In looking at this process we will focus on how we receive initial information, how we process that information, and how we ultimately reach a conclusion.

Another approach to understanding the *Feeling* skill is to view it as the combination of factors, including:

- The use of expressiveness to make connection with the environment
- A strong correlation with right-brain behavior
- The use of global thinking in decision making

In many ways, this combination produces a distinctly affective approach to decision making. It encourages connecting with the environment to maximize right-brain stimulation, and it results in global thinking.

Understanding through Contrast:

The groundbreaking work of Roger Sperry and Robert Ornstein on left and right brain dominance has allowed us to understand these different decision making processes. In the case of the *Feeling* skill, it is more right-brain dominance. Reviewing the contrast between right-brain and left-brain decision making can help us draw a distinction between *Thinking* and *Feeling* skills.

Thinking – Left-Brain Decision Making Process

The logic process outlined in this section describes our most commonly accepted understanding of the decision making process. In our western culture this is described as "rational decision making." It is logical and linear in nature. It moves through a "logical process" from beginning to end, using fact and rational analysis to arrive at conclusions. Below is a simplified example of this process.

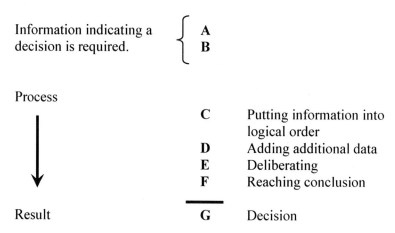

Information indicating a decision is required.	**A**	
	B	
Process		
	C	Putting information into logical order
	D	Adding additional data
	E	Deliberating
	F	Reaching conclusion
Result	**G**	Decision

Feeling – Right-Brain Decision Making Process

The *Feeling* approach to decision making is in many ways a more subtle and complex process. It relies strongly on one's experience base and is more intuitive in nature. On the following page is a simplified example of this complex process.

As you will note, right-brain thinking is a more comprehensive and complex way to think compared to the more linear, sequential, left-brain process. This is important to emphasize since there has been a strong inclination in our culture to discount the validity of the *Feeling* (right-brain) decision-making process. Acknowledging the validity of a method of reaching conclusions based on our personal data bank, one that is rooted in our past experience, may help the more logical among us better appreciate the *Feeling* skill.

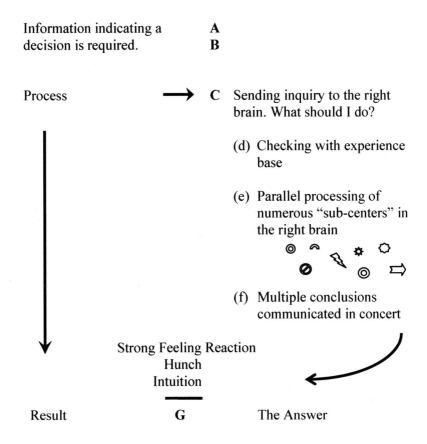

Information indicating a decision is required. **A**
B

Process   ⟶   C   Sending inquiry to the right brain. What should I do?

(d) Checking with experience base

(e) Parallel processing of numerous "sub-centers" in the right brain

(f) Multiple conclusions communicated in concert

Strong Feeling Reaction
Hunch
Intuition

Result   **G**   The Answer

The Feeling Skill – Described

Characteristic behaviors that are indicative of the *Feeling* skill include the following:

Reliance on sensory input as a primary basis of information gathering: People who are dominant in *Feeling* skill often report that the assemblage of facts is boring, and that it is an inefficient way to gain the necessary information for decision-making. Instead, they employ a wide range of sensory impressions. These include:

- Noting facial expressions or other non-verbal signals that are conveyors of information through nuance
- Quick scanning of written information to gain overview impressions
- Asking broad questions that provide opportunity for a wide range of responses

Once input is quickly gathered, the *Feeling* skilled person will spontaneously compare this information against other experiences. This comprehensive process provides the basis for their global thinking.

Trusting experience and intuitive messages: The person more dominant in the *Feeling* skill has a stronger inclination to acknowledge and act on intuitive impressions. As a point of contrast, having worked with a great many engineers over the years, I have found that they are clearly more *Thinking* dominant. When I ask about their response to these more intuitive hunches there is a common theme to their answers. They report: "It's not that I don't get hunches, but I don't tend to trust them and am not inclined to act on them." When I ask the same question to *Feeling* dominant people, they tell me that a trademark of their decision-making is listening to and responding to intuitive messages.

Seeing the big picture: Global thinking encourages a point of view that considers the whole, not parts. Accordingly, when using the *Feeling* skill, individuals want to move to the conclusion without being hampered by too many details. The result is a more big-picture point of view.

Non-Verbal Indicators

All of the non-verbal behaviors described in this section can be best understood as activities that precipitate right-brain behavior. These actions serve the purpose of generating a sense of personal energy, as well as creating a connection with the external environment. Observing these behaviors will help you recognize when someone is functioning with their *Feeling* skill.

Movement: One of the most prominent signals identifying the *Feeling* skill is movement. This may take the form of moving the hands and arms; it may be seen in gestures such as tapping a pencil or patting one's foot; it may include the need to walk around, or not staying still or seated for long periods. Whatever the movement, it serves the purpose of stimulating that more sensory part of us, and encourages *Feeling* skill activity. People who are very dominant in *Feeling* skill are sometimes perceived as being restless or inattentive due to the amount of movement they display when engaged in an interaction. In fact, for that individual, movement is simply a way to stay in touch.

Broad use of gestures: Predominantly *Feeling* skilled people are inclined to use more expansive gestures than do their *Thinking* skilled counterparts. As a rule of thumb, *Feeling* types will more often use gestures that go beyond the width of the body. Broad gestures with the arms held out wide or held up high are common. The number of hand and arm movements may also be exaggerated.

The *Thinking* type, in contrast, will more often use gestures from the elbows into the center of the body, gestures that are more limited and restricted.

Eye scanning: Looking at a wide variety of objects rather than limiting the visual field stimulates us and prompts more *Feeling,* or right-brain activity.

Proximity: The *Feeling* skilled person is more comfortable with a smaller zone of personal body space. This person can allow you to enter his or her personal space and be less distracted or disconcerted by that movement. People being in closer proximity may actually be a positive stimulation.

Touch: An extension of proximity is touch. *Feeling* types will utilize touch as a means of connection with others, and they will experience appropriate touching as a positive attribute.

Spontaneity: When *Feeling* types make the "intuitive leaps" described earlier, they will often respond with a kind excitement and freedom that is spontaneous.

Expressiveness: The energy with which they discuss things will often involve strong expressions of emotion. This expressiveness may manifest itself in words that are more emotion-laden. For example, the *Feeling* type is more likely to respond with a comment such as, "Wow, terrific, fantastic," than with one such as, "That's interesting."

The Feeling Skill – Misused

There are certain behaviors that are clearly a misuse of each of the skills. In most cases, this results from overuse of the preferred skill, or from a refusal to engage in the opposite skill behavior. I have identified some of the classic misuses of the *Feeling* skill below. Understanding these can be helpful in relating to people with this preferred skill.

Ignoring data: Since the *Feeling* type is so comfortable gaining information through sensory and experiential means, there is a strong temptation to avoid the discipline necessary to work their way through data that, in many cases, must be taken into account.

A clear example is balancing a checking account; there is simply no substitute for going through the data to arrive at an accurate number. I once interviewed the daughter of a CEO who was about to complete her undergraduate degree and was at a point of career decision. It was evident in the interview that she had a very strong preference for using the *Feeling* skill. When I asked her a question about handling money, she replied, "I haven't balanced my checkbook in the four years I've been at school. I have a sense of when I am about to run out of money, but it's based on impression. I don't know for sure, and I don't want to worry with the details." What she did not know was that her father, who was also on the account, was inquiring regularly and made a deposit if she appeared to be in danger of an overdraft. He resorted to this course of action after her third overdraft. Most of us will not have this luxury!

Unawareness of personal space: The *Feeling* skill creates a comfort level with closer proximity than others feel. When taken to an extreme, this can result in the person not recognizing when they have moved too close into another person's space. This behavior can produce socially awkward situations, causing the other party to become so ill at ease that they may want to avoid personal contact in the future.

Impulsiveness: Those who have not developed a good base of experience, or who depend too much on initial sensory input, do not take the time to do adequate global thinking. This is one of the most common complaints concerning the misuse of the *Feeling* skill, and can lead to decisions that are costly in terms of money, lost time, or hurt feelings. In short, they are unwilling to make proper inquiry of the right-brain experience base and are prone to impulsivity.

Discounting the counterpoint skill: When taken to an extreme, the *Feeling* type will tend to discount the more theoretical approach as cumbersome, stuffy, or as taking too much time. It is tempting for these individuals to make disparaging remarks such as, "What's taking those people so long to decide? The answer is obvious." Discounting the *Thinking* skill creates an attitude that discourages others who use that counterpoint method.

Over-expressiveness: When overdone, a good, healthy exuberance can become extreme to a point that is personally uncomfortable for some, and socially inappropriate for many. This may take the form of overly intense emotional reactions, or of overly energetic verbal expression.

Quick escape into boredom: It can become a destructive habit for *Feeling* skill people to lapse into boredom in situations when a lot of analytical thinking is required. This is much more likely to happen in a group problem-solving activity where they can mentally "drop out."

Reflection on the Feeling Skill

Listening to a bright, young technocrat attempt to reduce a complex interpersonal problem to a mathematical equation reinforced my belief that some problems go beyond the normal constraints of traditional logic. The more feeling, experiential, intuitive process adds an important dimension. This approach cuts through a great deal of extraneous information and gets right to the heart of the matter.

When we can trust this complex and somewhat mysterious process, the results can produce a sense of rightness that borders on epiphany. When in this mode we experience:

- The intuitive leap
- The juxtaposition of opposites into a larger form of agreement
- The synthesis of complex nuances into a meaningful whole
- Countless bits of information being stored in our unconscious to provide a basis for our decisions
- A natural effortlessness
- An excitement connected with a feeling of rhythm and rightness
- A sense of release when the intuitive choice becomes clear

At one time or another, each of us has awakened from a dream and been amazed at the ability of the unconscious to produce such powerful constructs. The closest our waking minds come to this broad-based, complex process is through paying attention to our intuition.

Maybe an early sign of respect for the intuitive messages we receive occurs when we first say to ourselves, "trust your hunch on this one." So the next time you hear that insistent, internal voice, you know what to do!

Personal Reflection

1. How willing am I to trust my hunches? What has been my history in this regard?

2. Are there places where I could adjust my use of the *Feeling* skill to better advantage?

INTERPERSONAL TECHNOLOGY ROADMAP

THE EIGHT KEY SKILLS

```
┌─────────────────────────────────────────────┐
│  SKILLS FOR EACH OF THE FOUR FACTORS          │
│            Defined & Described                │
└─────────────────────────────────────────────┘
                       │
                       ▼
┌─────────────────────────────────────────────┐
│       The Third Skill Set Relates To The      │
│             PRODUCT FACTOR                    │
└─────────────────────────────────────────────┘
```

PRODUCT *Factor:* How do we go about completing tasks? How do we implement decisions?

<u>Two Polar Opposite Skills</u>

    Choicing   ⟵⟶   **Dreaming**

Chapter 6

INTERPERSONAL TECHNOLOGY

THE FIFTH KEY SKILL

"CHOICING"

Defined, Described, Explored

FRED SHULTZ

One Of

EIGHT REMARKABLE PEOPLE

The Choicing Skill

He who stands outside the door already has a good part of his journey behind him.

-Dutch Proverb

A Brief Portrait

Sometime in our lives, most of us have had the experience of being in situations so out of character that we exclaim to ourselves, "This just doesn't compute." That is exactly the reaction I had the first time I entered Meridian Technology Center. It was supposed to be an educational institution, but everything I saw and heard made me question that definition. From the immaculate appearance of carpeted hallways and classrooms, to the way people talked about their work, this place looked and sounded like many of the major corporate headquarters I visit. I came to understand very quickly that I was not the only one surprised by this striking difference. Clearly, something distinctive and different was going on here.

Over the next several years as I continued to work in a consulting role with the school, my first impression was reinforced again and again. It was demonstrated in the manner in which the organization clearly exceeded the traditional role of vocational and technical education. They were not in the business of simply providing classes and waiting for students to attend. An example of that difference was evident when the outboard motor people, Mercruiser, announced they were considering moving to the Stillwater, Oklahoma area. The Meridian Technology staff immediately went to work identifying areas of required competence for those who would be employed in a manufacturing facility of that type. Once identified, they arranged to build a facility, install the specialized equipment required, and equipped themselves to train a new work force. This initiative was one of the contributing factors in Mercruiser's final decision to locate the plant in this community.

Meridian Technology's leadership in business and industry education has gone beyond meeting the needs of specific customers. It has become a regional business beacon by hosting conferences each year that bring leading business educators to the region. This has included such individuals as Warren Bennis, Richard Koestenbaum, Joel Barker, and Peter Block.

However, the distinction of functioning beyond the traditional norms of educational institutions is not only demonstrated in the way the staff works with their clients; it is apparent in the way they function within the institution. That includes such factors as performance-based pay, a strong program in professional development, and a high expectation for professionalism.

These and many other factors have made Meridian Technology an educational institution that is regularly visited by guests from all over the world, who come for the express purpose of getting a look at just how the school achieves these outstanding results.

Clearly, this surprising phenomenon did not happen by accident. While it has taken the commitment and dedication of many professionals, the driving force behind the success is the school's founding superintendent, Dr. Fred Shultz.

While Fred has a number of characteristics that have produced these remarkable results, his creative use of the *Choicing* skill has been instrumental in the achievement of this goal. Unlike many educators, he is not only able to generate creative ideas and to see the value of others' good ideas; he is able to bring them to fruition. His strong use of the *Choicing* skill allows him to act on ideas with decisiveness and consistency.

His need to see decisions made in a timely fashion, and to identify the most practical and pragmatic way to achieve the desired goal, has allowed Fred to move forward on programs while others are still considering the consequences. Fred has an uncanny ability to see what will be required for an initiative to be successful, and he will ensure that the people who are put in charge have the resources required to achieve that success.

One of the ways others experience this *Choicing* skill at work is when Fred begins to ask questions about a project in progress. Those who are not on track with a project will find his questions devastatingly on target. They cut to the essence of what will be necessary to get back on track or to move forward.

This more practical and concrete approach prompts Fred to notice the stain caused by a rusting light fixture on an exterior wall, or to see the flaw in a financial proposal with equal ease. In other words, the *Choicing* skill drives him to make sure both the concrete and the abstract issues that need to be covered are addressed.

The description I have provided could be misconstrued, leading some to think good *Choicing* skill is no more than managing concrete details. That would be selling the value of this skill far short. In Fred's case, it has meant that he had a dream of developing an educational institution that can make a difference, one that can make an impact on the lives of people and on the community. He has turned that dream into a reality by making educated choices, by keeping others focused on the task, and by accepting nothing less than exceptional results.

Recently, I served as a group facilitator for thirty members of the professional staff of Meridian Technology. They had come together to consider restructuring their organization. This group was comprised of top administrators, department heads, teachers, and even the intern who is a part of their professional development effort. Seeing every person participate, hearing the diversity of opinions, and experiencing the energy in the group, were all reminders of how bringing talented people together and providing the structure for them to perform were choices made by a wise and seasoned leader. Good *Choicing* skill is choosing sound options and acting on them in a practical and sense-making way. No one I know does this better than Dr. Fred Shultz.

The Choicing Skill – Defined

The *Choicing* skill is one of the two key skills we can use once a decision has been made and a course of action is required. It is the shift from deciding <u>what</u> we are going to do (which occurs at the "Path" stage), to determining <u>how</u> we are going to get it done. At this point, we have arrived at the "Product" stage of the process. The *Choicing* skill takes the position that making a definitive choice is imperative. The counterpoint skill of "*Dreaming,*" which we will discuss in the next chapter, emphasizes the importance of expanding the options and exploring possibilities. The *Choicing* skill takes a more direct approach, and encourages choices that create closure and produce end results.

The *Choicing* function focuses on concrete and specific results. While new ideas and new concepts in themselves can be an end product of considerable value, the more *Choicing* person will not be content with the development of a concept; he or she will immediately begin to ask how to turn exciting new ideas into useful and serviceable products.

The Choicing Skill – Described

As we begin to review some of the traits of the *Choicing* skill, it is important to remember that these characteristics, used appropriately, are strengths and are meant to be viewed in a positive light. The following are some of the key characteristics of the *Choicing* skill.

Making concrete observations: *Choicing* people will naturally concern themselves with specific outcomes. They are more likely to ask, "What is happening in this present situation?" "What will work best if we make a change?" "What is the best way to go about implementing this process?" Noticing exactly what is occurring is one asset that makes the *Choicing* person effective in implementing tasks.

Connecting concept and activity: Going through the mental steps to develop a way to move from idea to tangible result is the second major activity of a *Choicing* person. It is what allows them to be so effective in taking the sound ideas of others, and translating them into useful products.

Using reality checks: The *Choicing* person finds it natural to keep asking if an idea will really work, and what will be required to make the idea work in the specific situation. This constant questioning of the viability of an idea sometimes results in the *Choicing* person being labeled as negative. Their questioning, however, serves as a useful check for themselves and others.

The drive for closure: Once a decision has been made, the natural reaction of one dominant in the *Choicing* skill is to quickly shrink the options and choose a course of action. They will find it frustrating to continue to explore options once they believe they have determined a reasonable way to address the problem.

Practical and Concrete: The *Choicing* type's strong sensory awareness allows them to view things in a highly practical manner. They will seek the most commonsense approach to solve a problem, and will act on that choice.

Pragmatic: The definition of pragmatism as "the choice of a workable solution to meet an immediate problem" is an apt description of one quality of the *Choicing* skill. Rather than wait for consideration of all possible solutions, selecting one that meets the criteria of solving the immediate problem is adequate. The individual may understand that this choice may not be the perfect solution in the long term, but if it does not cause harm and will not actually cause a problem in the future, the *Choicing* type will feel free to act on the solution.

Timeliness: The strong sensory awareness of *Choicing* people gives them a keener sense of how long a project is likely to take. This characteristic enables them to set realistic timelines for a project.

Results oriented: The high need to produce an end product is one of the drivers that comes naturally to the *Choicing* skill. Seeing measurable results is gratifying for these individuals.

Balancing the cost-benefit equation: The *Choicing* person is more aware than others that turning concepts into realities is not free. As a result of this heightened awareness, they will make certain that the cost of producing the desired end does not outweigh the benefit.

Non-Verbal Indicators

Some of the behaviors that can help you know when an individual is exercising the *Choicing* skill are listed in the next several paragraphs. An overall set of behaviors that are key indicators of *Choicing* activity involve downward motion.

Anchoring: When in the midst of exercising choice, it is not uncommon for them to strike their fist into the palm of the other hand and to exclaim, "SOLD!" That gesture feels and looks right. It would be hard to imagine, on the other hand, someone throwing their hands up into the air and shouting "SOLD!" We are much more likely to throw our hands in the air when things are unsettled and we are frustrated about it. That is just the opposite of anchoring. Another example of anchoring is banging the gavel to close a meeting. These are decisive downward gestures.

Emphasis: This non-verbal behavior is similar to anchoring, but is a less dramatic expression. This might take the form of ticking off items on our fingers when we have points to make, or listing issues that have been decided.

Voice inflection: A common indicator of *Choicing* skill is hearing the last syllable of a sentence voiced lower and given slightly stronger emphasis. For example, if a *Choicing* person was taking questions from a group, and had decided he or she did not want any more, the person might cut off questions with a non-verbal signal. They could ask a question with a lowering of tone and increase in volume on the last word, such as: "Any more <u>questions</u>."↓ Despite the words spoken, the non-verbal message is, "I don't want any more questions." That means of delivering the message is often quite effective.

Well Grounded Stance: The need to be practical, concrete, and down-to-earth is expressed by the individual placing the feet firmly on the ground. There is very little tendency to shift or move about. Planting the feet so firmly in position signals that the person has made a choice, has "taken a stand."

A number of years ago, the owner of a jewelry store shared an observation that demonstrates how often the *Choicing* skill can be identified through this planting of the feet. Through keen observation, he had discovered that customers looking at jewelry will often stand at the case and lift one foot, leaving only the toe on the ground. Standing behind the person, almost the entire sole of the shoe is visible, as only the point of the toe remains on the ground.

Or, they will shift from side to side while looking at the many possible choices before them. Once they decide on an item they like, however, they take a firm, solid stance with both feet planted. It was at this moment that the owner would, as if by magic, pick the perfect time to ask, "Is there something I could show you?"

Impatience with exploration: Once the *Choicing* type has chosen an option for how to complete a task, he/she will have little patience with continued exploration of other potential courses of action. Now that the bottom line is in view, the *Choicing* type sees any further consideration as a waste of time. This impatience will often take the form of non-verbal "hurry-up" signals, such as facial expressions signaling disapproval, tapping the table rapidly, or sighing.

The Choicing Skill – Misused

As we indicated in the introduction of the *Choicing* skill descriptions, these skills are strengths when use appropriately. Unfortunately, they can also be misused. Some of the most common misuses are discussed in this section, and are provided as a checkpoint or warning for how we can wrongly use this very helpful skill.

The most common misuse of the *Choicing* skill involves overvaluing the practical point of view. The eight behaviors described below represent the most frequent examples I have observed in the workplace.

Closing off ideas: When a work group is in a brainstorming mode, one of the common misuses of the *Choicing* skill occurs when the person "rains on the ideas" that others propose. They are likely to point out that there are enough ideas to work with already, and it is wasting time continuing to produce more. This blocking of ideas can also occur through the use of overly blunt questions.

Disparaging creativity: The overly zealous *Choicing* person may describe creativity as unrealistic, wasteful, and unnecessary. There are times when this attack on creativity is done through sarcasm.

Over-simplifying processes: In an attempt to be efficient, the *Choicing* person will seek to keep things simple. They are often the ones to use the "KISS" (keep it simple, stupid) phrase. However, in the drive for simplicity, they will sometimes cut out important steps in a process or an interaction. This cutting out the "fluff," as they see it, can be disastrous to the original intent of a process.

Hiding behind cost issues: If misused, *Choicing* skill can result in resorting to cost as a rationale, when in fact it is only resistance to an idea that is prompting their objection.

Alienating oneself from more innovative individuals: Consistent misuse of the *Choicing* skill in the ways described above can offend innovative people in the work environment. The loss of these people's ideas and input can be costly.

Unwillingness to revisit an idea: One counterproductive expression of *Choicing* skill is the habit of pronouncing an idea dead, and being unwilling to consider it again. There are times when an idea that was not workable three years ago may come to fruition today. Refusal to revisit ideas solely because they were considered in the past raises the prospect of overlooking important strategic advantages. A common quote connected with this misuse of the *Choicing* skill is, "We've already tried that."

Refusal to explore sufficient options: I coined the word, *"Choicing,"* to indicate a strong need to make choices. However, when taken to an extreme, this tendency can cut off consideration of options and thereby result in <u>poor</u> choices.

Overconfidence in the practical approach: Because there are so many instances where making a decisive choice results in success, it is tempting to assume that every situation calls for this practical approach. It is somewhat akin to the observation, "If the only resource you have is a nail, every solution seems to call for a hammer."

A Reflection on the Choicing Skill

Edward de Bono, researcher and writer on creative thinking, explains much when he reveals how the mind works. He speaks to all of us when he describes our discomfort with uncertainty. As he says, if we find ourselves lost while traveling in a large city, we are distressed until we get back on track. We need to feel a sense of the familiar. He speaks of what we all have experienced – "dis-ease" in the face of uncertainty.

When we face a new and different project, or must decide how to accomplish a new challenge, we come to that moment when we must make a choice. What is the best way? What will produce the best result? What to do?

It is only as we choose a course of action that we can feel ourselves back on track. Once the means of accomplishing the task is settled upon, we can experience a sense of assurance. It feels like:

- Having a sense of direction
- Being settled
- Moving forward
- Being practical
- Getting things accomplished
- Being effective

It is very positive and self-affirming to make a choice that produces wholeness and completion, and lets us announce with a sense of self-satisfaction, "Done!"

Personal Reflection

How do I react when it is time to make a choice?

How satisfied am I with my use of the *Choicing* skill?

Are there shifts I need to make that would help me be more effective?

Chapter 7

INTERPERSONAL TECHNOLOGY

THE SIXTH KEY SKILL

"DREAMING"

Defined, Described, Explored

JOE STOUGH

One Of

EIGHT REMARKABLE PEOPLE

The Dreaming Skill

A moment's insight is worth a life's experience.

-Oliver Wendell Holmes

A Brief Portrait

Meeting Joe Stough, the founder of Syntex Management Solutions, five years ago was somewhat like walking into an intellectual thunderstorm. Ideas flashed onto the scene like lightening bolts, followed by the thunderclap of the implications of those ideas for the business. Joe was an intellectual phenomenon of the information age. Creativity crackled in the air.

During our first coaching session, it was clear that Joe's vision had spawned a business that was growing at such a rate that it was a managerial challenge for him and the staff. What was also clear was that Joe's natural inclination was toward visionary leadership, not toward management detail. His remarkable visioning had brought the company to the point where they were striving to keep abreast of the requests for services, nearly all coming from some of the most prestigious fortune five hundred companies.

Over the next several months, working with Joe only emphasized how his use of the *Dreaming* skill was a key factor in his success. It started when, as a student athlete at USC, he saw a need for a record keeping system for the baseball team and created a computer program to meet that need. Years later, he duplicated that experience while developing sophisticated software that tracks management and safety processes and provides templates that are amazingly intuitive in both tracking and predicting processes.

Joe's genius, however, has not simply been developing his ideas into productive software programs. It has been his ability to translate those ideas in a way that people can grasp them and catch a sense of the possibilities implied. I do not consider myself technically savvy, but when Joe becomes excited while explaining what his product can do, I find myself following along and understanding. I even find myself becoming excited, too. What I experience is apparently what happens to customers when Joe talks with them about Syntex Solutions, because they certainly respond!

In 2003, I had the privileged of nominating Joe for the Ernst and Young Entrepreneur of the Year Award. I was not surprised in the least when he won. He fits the description perfectly.

The Dreaming Skill – Defined

The *Dreaming* skill represents one of the two major approaches we take in acting on decisions once they are made. People dominant in *Dreaming* skill behavior often respond to a new decision as the beginning of an exploration. This is in sharp contrast to the *Choicing* person, who views a decision as an invitation to choose a course of action and move on.

For the *Dreaming* person, the task at hand is not necessarily the only activity to be considered. It is very important to the *Dreaming* person to generate new ideas, new concepts, or new opportunities. It is not merely a matter of getting something done; it is a matter of improving the <u>method</u> of getting something done while reaching that goal.

In contrast with pragmatism, *Dreaming* centers on creativity and on making a contribution to improved processes. The *Dreaming* skill is <u>future-focused</u>, looking at what *can be* rather than what *has been*.

The Dreaming Skill – Described

There are a number of obvious behaviors that help us identify an individual who is operating in the *Dreaming* mode. You may well recognize these behaviors in yourself, or in others in your personal or professional sphere.

Consistent expansion of options: Once a decision is made, the need to implement the decision is the next apparent step. For the person predominate in *Dreaming* skill, the first natural reaction is to explore the options before taking action. The *Dreaming* individual is not simply looking for a course of action; they are looking for the *best* course of action or solution. The mere act of generating numerous approaches or strategies is rewarding for this person.

A good example of expanding options is the commonplace exercise of brainstorming. For the person dominant in *Dreaming* skill, this activity is energizing and gratifying. It is a chance to do what they do best. There are others who, due to their dominant skill of *Choicing*, will find it difficult to engage in a lot of brainstorming.

Appreciates the theoretical: If you are a *Dreaming* type, you recognize that practical concerns are worthwhile, and there will be a point at which you are ready to move to the implementation phase. However, you are likely to be very aware that it is the generation of new and fresh concepts that launch new enterprises, and that helps old ones take new shape and regain momentum. This viewpoint results in a higher value being placed on the theoretical than will be the case for your more practical counterparts.

Creativity is valued: It is not merely the number of ideas or options generated that matters to the *Dreaming* skilled person. It is also the depth and originality of ideas that counts. Creativity, when defined as ideas that are novel and at the same time useful, is what is most appreciated. What *Dreaming* skilled people really value and consider worthwhile is not reviewing numerous ideas that have already been recognized and explored; what they value is a refreshing, intriguing new idea.

Lateral logic is more common: Edward de Bono, in his important work on mental processes, planted the seed for the popular phrase, "thinking outside the box." This skill represents the capacity to make the mental leap from one track of thinking to a different plane, usually when it is least expected. This ability to move beyond the obvious to a new line of thinking is reflective of the *Dreaming* skill.

Moving beyond the immediate task: Once an idea has surfaced or a concept is proposed, it is natural for the *Dreaming* person to follow that idea to its many possible conclusions. This includes exploring implications that may not obviously apply to the task at hand. Nevertheless, they may make an unexpected connection that produces fruitful results.

Prone toward potential: *Dreaming* skilled individuals tend to consider the potential of an idea. This results in their being inclined to think about future possibilities. Coming up with new approaches, new applications, or new directions are all a natural part of this person's mode of operation.

Venture capitalists: The *Dreaming* skill person is not the traditional venture capitalist in the sense of providing funding, but they are often the ones who come up with a concept that inspires others to move into a new arena. They are what I sometimes describe as conceptual catalysts. They make things happen through their creative contribution to the process.

Non-Verbal Indicators

The *Dreaming* skill encourages development of options and exploration of concepts. As a result, the bodily postures and non-verbal actions related to this skill generate an openness to possibility and a responsiveness to things creative. I will share some of the most obvious behaviors that can help you identify when a person is engaging in *Dreaming* activity.

Upward movement: Anything that will foster continued openness is likely to be displayed by a *Dreaming* person. This will mean not using physical behaviors that shut off options, such as a downward gesture that suggests closure. Instead, the person will likely exhibit numerous upward gestures with the arms or hands. This will often include turning the palms upward when conversing with another person.

Upward eye movement: When exploring an idea or a concept and searching for the implications of an idea, the *Dreaming* individual may glance upward as a means of stimulating the generation of new ideas. Anyone who has been observant while sitting through lectures in a university has probably noticed this behavior.

Rising voice inflection: *Dreaming* skilled individuals will often express ideas with the use of upward inflection at the end of a sentence. This gives emphasis to the open-ended aspect of the subject, and suggests that further exploration of the thought is expected. This will particularly be the case when the topic is especially exciting or challenging.

Floating Gait: There is a clear need for the *Dreaming* person to avoid becoming stuck in uncreative pathways. Their not placing the foot too firmly on the ground is evidence of that need. In the *Dreaming* mode, these individuals will often walk more on the balls of their feet than on the heels. When standing still, the person is also more likely to shift slightly in order not to become too "earthbound." These people may be observed actually rising up on their toes when giving a speech, especially when the idea they are sharing is extremely exciting to them.

The Dreaming Skill – Misused

Every skill has its Achilles heel, and in the case of the *Dreaming* skill, the major element of misuse centers on *theory over practice.* You can observe this in the following examples:

Tendency to reinvent: It is often difficult to get the *Dreaming* dominant individual to let go of a process once it has reached a reasonable conclusion. Instead, the person may insist on continuing to tinker with a new design, to want to make small changes after everyone else has already concluded that the product or process put in place is sufficient.

Discounting practicality: Because *Dreaming* people see the theoretical as paramount, they sometimes tend to discount practicality as being simplistic. This often leads them to ignore important details, and become known as an "absent-minded professor."

Love affair with theory: From my time living and working around a university, I recall one colleague who held a theory contrary to everyone else in his field. It was interesting to see how he could find ingenious ways to bring up the issue even though others were clearly dealing with unrelated matters. Over time, his clinging to the theory became not so much a novelty as an eccentricity, and finally became a burden for others to bear.

Ignoring important timelines: The *Dreaming* person in pursuit of new insight may lose touch with the fact that the current situation demands they move out of exploration and into production. Ignoring deadlines and being surprised when others are irritated is not uncommon for the person who ignores the present in favor of the future.

A Reflection on the Dreaming Skill

When I think of the *Dreaming* skill I think of potential, the power of the mind, the power of an idea. I have found no better way to illustrate that potential than through the poem by T.E. Lawrence, who speaks of the phenomenon in this way:

> All people dream, but not equally.
> Those who dream by night
> in the dusty recesses of their mind
> wake in the day to find that it was vanity.
> But the dreamers of the day
> are dangerous people
> for they may act on their dream with open eyes
> to make it possible.

Personal Reflection

1. How well am I using my capacity for creativity?

2. What could I do that would make this a more productive skill for me?

3. Is this a skill that I need to emphasize or to curb?

INTERPERSONAL TECHNOLOGY ROADMAP

THE EIGHT KEY SKILLS

SKILLS FOR EACH OF THE FOUR FACTORS

Defined & Described

↓

The Fourth Skill Set Relates To The

PACE FACTOR

PACE *Factor:* What is my preferred rate of activity? How does my natural cadence affect and influence the three other factors?

<u>Two Polar Opposite Skills</u>

$$\text{Active} \longleftrightarrow \text{Pensive}$$

Chapter 8

INTERPERSONAL TECHNOLOGY

THE SEVENTH KEY SKILL

"ACTIVE"

Defined, Described, Explored

DENNIS HARRIS

One Of

EIGHT REMARKABLE PEOPLE

The Active Skill

A Brief Portrait

One thing I have learned while watching people's career advancement over the past two decades is that unless you own the building, there is no elevator to success. You have to take the stairs. Dennis Harris, a former executive at SBC, takes the steps two at a time. There are many people who achieve remarkable results in the workplace, but considerably fewer who do so in surprisingly short time frames. When reflecting upon what has enabled Dennis to move up the ladder of success, there is no one factor that can be isolated as the sole ingredient.

In Dennis' case, it appears to be a combination of caring about others, being committed to the organization, having a sense of vision, and seeing how to accomplish that vision. However, underlying all these characteristics is a sense of urgency, a need for speed, which keeps him ahead of the pack. It is this *Pace* factor that sets him apart from many others. His need for action is not wasted on random activity. It is translated into focused activity that produces outstanding achievements.

I have often asked myself why it is so difficult to achieve remarkable results in large organizations. Why is it so hard to make things happen rapidly? One explanation is what I call the "drag factor." It is a built in inertia resulting from a natural resistance to change – the larger the organization, the heavier the drag. Many of the things we now describe as hallmark achievements were first labeled impossible. Even when we do not label new initiatives impossible, we have tendency to define them as unrealistic or too difficult.

For those with a strong drive for action, these milestones appear much more achievable than they do to most people. Dennis's high-energy, high-action approach gives him a comfort level with demanding goals. It also helps him lead in a manner that overcomes the natural organizational inertia that slows down progress. A key element of his success is Dennis's ability to convey his comfort and confidence in others and in their capacity to accomplish remarkable results.

During the years when he served as general manager of Southwestern Bell Telephone for the Dallas, Fort Worth, Austin, and West Texas Region, I watched this market area make remarkable strides. The progress included a broad range of improvements, including enhanced operational efficiency, developing more positive labor relations, and greater customer satisfaction.

Having employees describe their amazement at what was accomplished in such a short time is a testament to leadership that highlighted rapid response and solid results.

After serving as President of the Mid-West Region for SBC, Dennis retired to an active life as a consultant. I recently had the privilege of having him work with Panhandle Energy as a consultant on union relationships. Watching the energy that his active approach generated with the senior management team was further testament to how this skill has served Dennis so well.

The Active Skill – Defined

The *Active* skill reflects the preferred pace of individuals as they engage in the other skill sets (Self-Motivated/Other-Motivated, Thinking/Feeling, Choicing/Dreaming). In many ways, the *Active* skill is a primary influencing factor in how the other skills are expressed. For example, a person with a strong preference for *Active* behavior who is also *Other-Motivated* will want to develop relationships quickly. They will be less inclined to exercise caution or be hesitant about entering into relationships with others.

In defining the *Active* skill, there a number of factors that can help you recognize when someone is operating from this preferred pace.

Highly confident with taking action: These people experience action-taking as second nature, so while others wait, they will have already moved forward. All of us have seen those coffee mugs with the Latin inscription, "Carpe Diem" (Seize the Day). No one seems to understand that saying better than people with *Active* skill dominance. Their sense of urgency and their preference for rapid action allows them to recognize and to *act* when an opportunity presents itself.

Has a sense of internal urgency: A part of the drive to action comes from their internal sense of urgency. They find it difficult to slow down, even when others suggest it might be helpful for them.

In many cases, slowing down is not actually helpful for these people. All that happens is that their stress level rises, because they are not responding to the call to action generated by their sense of internal urgency. For some people, telling them to "slow down" is well intended, but is the wrong advice.

Rapid movement: Preference for activity is usually combined with rapid physical movement. If the person does not exhibit rapid physical movement, they may replace the physical need for action with rapid speech patterns. Not only are *Active* skilled individuals likely to speak more rapidly, they encourage rapid interchange in their dialogue with you. They do so through their own quick responses, and their look of expectation that telegraphs that they want you to response with equal alacrity. You will likely have your best conversations with the *Active* skilled person when you are quick and energetic in your own responses.

High energy: While there is not an absolute correlation between a high preference for action taking and a high energy level, the two often go hand in hand.

Multi-task approach: People high in the need for action taking usually are not satisfied with being involved in one thing at a time. They are much more inclined to engage in multiple tasks or projects and to be stimulated by the activity level.

Goal-oriented: Making things happen is integrally linked to setting goals and milestones. Having targets seems to be a way of encouraging focus and intensity for the *Active* skilled person.

Often appears restless: Since this individual's pace is more active than the general population, they will often find it difficult to sit through meetings they believe should be completed more promptly, or to wait for a decision to be reached when they have already mentally moved though the process. Others may sometimes confuse their restlessness for inattentiveness or disagreement. It is important to understand their restlessness as part of a *pace* factor, rather than as approval or disapproval of the issue at hand.

Enjoys seeing others act promptly: The more *Active* person derives a sense of satisfaction from seeing others moving quickly into action. I have found that one of the complaints *Active* paced executives sometimes have about other managers is that they are not decisive enough. Often, what they are describing is a matter of preferred *pace*.

I have had the experience of working with two executives to help them develop a more productive relationship. The CEO is a fast-paced dealmaker. The other manager is less action-oriented and is a more analytical type. The task of the second manager is to serve as the team member who sizes up the deals, which are generally large and complex. As one might guess, for the dealmaker, the analysis is never fast enough, and for the analytical person, some of the deadlines appear artificial and prompted by the need for action rather than being real business needs. Being able to understand *pace* and to discuss their different preferences has produced a meaningful shift toward a healthy balance in their interactions.

Even though they have achieved a greater degree of balance, the CEO with the high *Active* skill will not find it easy to be comfortable with the more measured pace of the other manager, because the CEO's natural comfort base is with those who act promptly.

Moves to new topics while others are still processing the present one: It is somewhat disconcerting for those with a less *Active* pace to realize that their more action-prone colleague has moved to another topic while they are still discussing the previous one. Although it may be disconcerting, it is likely to happen anyway. This is the pace that feels natural for the *Active* dominant individual.

Plan on the fly: These people find it agonizing to sit through long and laborious meetings where others are struggling with developing plans. They are much more likely to plan while doing other things. *Active* dominant individuals often report doing planning on the drive to work, or while getting ready for work. They may even work on planning during meetings that require their presence, but which they consider unproductive.

Most of the time, when these individuals arrive for planning meetings they already have their part of the plan in mind. Oftentimes it is obvious to others that they have already reached some important conclusions. Rather than making them wait until the "proper time," it would be helpful to find ways to invite their input early on in the dialogue. Doing so can contribute to more efficient meetings, and it will also make them much more effective participants.

Brief meetings and interchanges: When *Active* dominant individuals are in charge of meetings, they will work to cover the topics as quickly as possible. They have to work hard to allow everyone the time they need to make their contributions. As a result, others often feel "cut off" in meetings. There are times when this can create misunderstandings with some members of a work group.

Need to "get things done": It is difficult for *Active* skilled people to refrain from moving quickly to the task at hand, since action takes precedence over other factors. An example of a person who managed to balance the need to relate and the need to take action was Charles McMahen, the past chairman of Compass Bank, Texas. He would visit with you in a very cordial and relaxed manner in order to establish connection. After that, without being abrupt he would make it clear that the time for idle chatter was over and he was ready to move to new territory. The result was that he was a very efficient manager, but he was also involved in numerous community affairs as well as organizational issues.

The Active Skill: Non-Verbal Indicators

The most obvious non-verbal indicators of the *Active* skill can be seen in three areas: 1) physical quickness, 2) demonstration of a need for action, and 3) movement. Each of these is discussed below.

Physical Quickness

All of us move rapidly when situations call for it. You can see this at any major airport as you watch people hurrying, obviously late for a flight. In the case of *Active* dominant individuals, however, rapid movement is their natural pace. This includes:

- Walking rapidly – These people walk at a rapid clip. When entering a room, for example, they will enter at a much more rapid pace than their less *Active* counterparts. You may notice a sense of briskness as they arrive.
- Abrupt gestures – The *Active* dominant person will have gestures that start and stop more abruptly. They will stab the air when making a point, for instance. These gestures begin quickly and end with energy. There is a distinct lack of smooth flow to their gestures.
- Rapid speech patterns – Although speech itself is verbal rather than non-verbal, the rate and pattern of speech is significant. The model that can be identified as more *Active* has to do with expression rate. When making a presentation, the rate is fast-paced, with a tendency to hit the beginning and ending of words hard. This makes for a rapid-fire, fast-clipped presentation. Similarly, when engaging in conversation, the *Active* person responds almost instantaneously.

Signaling the Need for Action

Their non-verbal behavior expresses an action orientation. However, the *Active* dominant individual will also use non-verbal behavior to encourage action on the part of others. The following are non-verbal cues that seek to prompt others into an action mode.

- "Hurry-up" gestures – There are a number of gestures that signal the person wants the speaker to move along. Gestures that may indicate a bit of impatience include drumming the fingers on the table, or tapping a pencil to suggest another person move to conclusion. A final "hurry-up" gesture involves abruptly nodding the head coupled with a facial expression indicating the person is harried and wants the other party to hurry along.

- Interruptions – A second clear indicator that is partially verbal, but has a number of non-verbal components, is the act of interrupting. In some cases, the interruption is verbal and may involve the *Active* dominant person finishing sentences for another person. Other times the break has less to do with content and simply serves to short-circuit conversation. They may do this with an interruption such as a decisive, "I UNDERSTAND!" The message is that the other party has taken too much time in discussion or explanation and is through.

- A more informal pattern involves the person giving a rapid burst of "yeah, yeah, yeah," which indicates that the other party is taking too much time and attention, and is expected to move on. If you happen to live in Texas where I reside, or in some other southern states, the "yeah" might be replaced with "yep, yep, yep" – a variation with the same intent.

- Leaving and returning to meetings – Everyone needs to leave a meeting from time to time, but for the *Active* dominant person the need is often much higher. When a meeting bogs down, their belief that doing something else will be more productive prompts them to exit and return later.

Movement

Some forms of movement help *Active* dominant people deal with the pressures of their internal drive for urgency.

- Pacing – The need for external action is high, and if the situation requires a limitation of action, the *Active* dominant person will experience greater stress than the average person. To relieve some of the stress, the person may resort to pacing when that is possible. If they cannot pace, they may tap the foot or use some other physical expression to reduce stress.

- Distraction – Similarly, the *Active* dominant person may be distracted by external activity, and will be tempted to join in any diversion that suggests an opportunity to release tension through physical activity. An example would be going over to join a lively and energetic group during the break time of a meeting.

Misuse of the Active Skill

Misuse of some skills is more noticeable than others, and this certainly applies in the case of the *Active* skill. Because this skill is so closely related to external activity, any misuse of the skill is highly visible and therefore painfully apparent.

You will probably find it easy to think of people and situations in which you have seen these behaviors. If you are more *Active* dominant yourself, perhaps you can identify with the behaviors first hand. I have listed below the most apparent behaviors I have commonly observed.

Action, action, and action only: Insisting that nothing good is happening unless some external activity is occurring prompts overly *Active* paced individuals to stir up situations or create unnecessary commotions. In the work setting, this behavior is sometimes manifested by the person creating crisis just to stimulate activity.

Multiple "number-one" priorities: An *Active* dominant person who misuses that skill often does so by blurring priorities. Every priority is deemed critical and must be acted upon immediately. This fosters an "emergency room" work or living environment, not only for themselves but for others as well. Many people can relate stories about a boss calling after hours or while they were on vacation, demanding that something must be done <u>right</u> <u>now</u>. The tyranny of needing everything completed immediately clearly becomes a major source of stress for all parties involved.

Low tolerance for reflection: It is difficult for the overly *Active* person to tolerate non-physical activity that is either not visible or is not immediately leading to overt activity. I recall years ago talking with an employee of IBM when their slogan was, "THINK." The person told me, "Even though I have that slogan posted on the wall directly in my line of sight, if my boss walks in and I am just sitting at my desk apparently doing nothing, it will not go over well if he asks what I'm doing and I reply, "I am thinking." In further discussion with the employee, it became clear that the boss was a living example of low tolerance for reflection.

Impulsive: The need for action can sometimes lead the overly *Active* person to move forward even when there is insufficient information, inadequate commitment from others, or when for numerous other reasons it may be precipitous to proceed. Their comfort level with activity prompts impulsivity.

Intellectual impatience: Liking to do things rapidly applies not only to physical activity, but also to mental activity. When making decisions, for example, the *Active* skilled person likes to move through information rapidly and make decisions quickly. As a result, an *Active* person who is also very bright will be more intellectually impatient with decision makers who take a more deliberate approach. Experiencing this impatience is both natural and unavoidable for *Active* individuals. It becomes a misuse, however, when they develop behaviors that outwardly signal their intellectual impatience to a degree that it becomes threatening or disruptive for others.

A Reflection on the Active Skill

What we value in our living and working experience alters with time and circumstance. A recent item I have noticed appearing on performance appraisal forms is a question concerning the employee's sense of urgency. Being known as decisive and action-oriented is high on the current corporate and community list of virtues. This is not difficult to understand when we think about how good it feels when we act quickly to attack a problem. When we do this, we can see ourselves as:

- Leaders
- Energetic
- Agile and quick
- Ahead of the curve

When we procrastinate, the results are often negative. We create a list of accusations that we use against ourselves in silent dialogue. Delay diminishes us. Hesitancy allows others unnecessary advantage. Indecisiveness robs us of an opportunity to lead. Making things happen, getting things started, can produce self-confidence in the face of daunting odds. So what are you waiting for?

Personal Reflection

1. How well do I manage my personal *Pace*?

2. If an adjustment is needed, is it in the direction of being more action oriented, or is it more a need to slow down and notice what is going on around me?

3. What can I do to assure the most effective use of the *Active* skill?

Chapter 9

"PENSIVE" SKILL

Defined, Described, Explored

DAN BUTCHER

One Of

EIGHT REMARKABLE PEOPLE

The Pensive Skill

A Brief Portrait

The final person I have chosen to highlight is not in keeping with my original intent only to use persons with whom I have worked. I have worked as a consultant with the seven prior persons, and have enough history to know them extremely well. In this case, I have also chosen someone I know very well, but at the risk of being accused of journalistic nepotism, I have chosen my son-in law, Dan Butcher.

As of this writing, Dan is the Managing Partner of Strasburger and Price law firm, with headquarters in Dallas, and offices in Houston, Austin, San Antonio, Frisco, Washington, D.C., New York City and Mexico City. However, Dan was already a member of our family when he joined the firm in 1984, and like most new employees, he began at the bottom.

I watched him go quietly to work in the tax department working long hours, meeting demanding goals. As was his nature, he was understated and unobtrusive in the manner in which went about his work. Nevertheless, with his *Pensive* skill he was observing and inquiring all the while, in preparation for making greater contributions to the firm.

It was obvious when I was with Dan at social and family gatherings that he often had little to say, but when he did speak, it was apparent that he had been giving considerable thought – and people listened.

Dan's ability to use the *Pensive* skill in planning and strategizing has been a natural asset in his career advancement. It has resulted in some breakthrough ideas that have benefitted both the firm and their clients.

From what I know secondhand, Dan is the kind of manager who does not allow himself to be stampeded into precipitous action in the face of an emotional request from a persuasive attorney. Instead, he takes the time to reflect and consider the alternatives before moving into action. His *Pensive* skill provides a natural balance in an environment that, by its nature, can become combative and impulsive.

When *Pensive* people engage in strategizing and planning for the future, most of the activity happens internally. It is a reflective process. As a result, in some instances it may appear to others that Dan lacks a sense of urgency. To make that assumption would be a costly mistake, because underneath that unrevealing exterior is a degree of conviction and passion that will produce powerful results.

Throughout his career, Dan has not been one to boast. Rather, he balances his insight and experience with his natural ability to strategize, and to chart a course for himself and those around him that is indeed remarkable.

The Pensive Skill – Described

Strategy based action: When operating in the *Pensive* mode, individuals prefer to take action based on a strategy. It is natural for the *Pensive* person to take time to create a strategy before moving into action. They are in many ways like a skillful chess player, plotting future moves before being willing to take the present one.

Investigation and evaluation: Observing and inquiring are trusted tools of *Pensive* people. The *Pensive*-skilled person is not comfortable entering a new situation and immediately making changes. Taking time to observe and gather information to create a change strategy is much more their style.

Resists pressure for immediate action: If it appears to *Pensive*-skilled people that they are being pressured to move too quickly, they will often use withdrawal or non-action to resist what feels to them to be hasty action. Though this behavior is sometimes perceived as being non-cooperative or non-responsive, it is more likely to be a reaction designed to allow adequate time for reflection.

Thrives in a quiet environment: A quiet environment is conducive to reflection, and is a natural fit for the *Pensive* person. They enjoy working in surroundings that offer minimal interruptions and few demanding deadlines. That setting provides the best opportunity to utilize their *Pensive* skill.

Exhibits patience: Since they prefer to operate at a less hurried pace, they are willing to allow others to do likewise. In consequence, they can be more patient with an individual who is taking time to consider a course of action. This patience may also make them a better listener, unless they fall into the habit of internally rehearsing their response while the other person is still talking.

Sees reflection as a positive tool: While the more *Active* person may have a tendency to label a *Pensive* person as lacking urgency, the *Pensive* person knows how important this skill has been in creating productive strategies. They also know the number of times it has helped them avoid a false start on an important project. As a result, they experience reflection as a valuable asset.

The Pensive Skill: Non-Verbal Indicators

There are a number of indicators that tell us a person is in a more *Pensive* mode. Most of these behaviors help create an environment which is more reflective. Here are some of the most common indicators:

Slightly slower gait: The *Pensive* skilled individual will enter a room in a more leisurely manner, not hurrying, neither stopping nor starting movement abruptly. In subtle ways their behavior will send messages that it is OK to slow down.

Relaxed or informal body positions: This individual will assume positions that are related to being more relaxed. This will include a greater tendency to slump, or to lean on furniture for support. They may also lean back in a very relaxed manner, or stretch out in a relaxed body extension when sitting.

Softer speaking voice: The voice will often be very well modulated, with less tendency to express themselves with emphasis. It is also not uncommon for this individual to use less volume than others when speaking.

Smoother gestures: The gestures seem to flow and be less abrupt or "jerky" than those of more intense and *Active* individuals.

Expressions of tolerance: The attitude of patience is expressed non-verbally as a signal of tolerance. The *Pensive* person will allow you more time to express yourself without showing impatience. The individual will encourage your own reflection by sending approval messages, such as positive facial expressions or head nods. They may even join in the reflective experience by being silently reflective themselves.

Longer periods of silence: This person can allow themselves time for reflection even when they are in the midst of a conversation with you. Do not be surprised when the silences are of greater duration than may be comfortable if you are not strongly *Pensive* yourself.

Misuse of Pensive Skill

Just because someone has a dominance of *Pensive* skill does not guarantee they will misuse the skill. As is the case with all of the skills, they are essentially positive in nature unless used in the extreme, at which time they often become a liability. Some of the danger signs indicating this has occurred in the use of *Pensive* behavior include the following:

Reflect, reflect, reflect!: When misused, reflection can become an end in itself. In those instances, the environment becomes something of a think tank. The result is never getting around to action.

Dodging the action: Allowing others to take action while remaining uninvolved can become a counterproductive habit.

Negative response to a call to action: Since their view is that quick action often leads to costly false starts, *Pensive* individuals may develop a strong mistrust of people who sound a call to action. When this becomes a knee-jerk reaction, there is a lack of discretion when the call to action is a legitimate response.

World's leading procrastinators: Taking more time than is necessary to review a situation can lead to a habit of procrastination.

Extreme introspection: In extreme cases, overuse of *Pensive* behavior can result in the individual becoming so introspective as to withdraw from relating in the here-and-now.

A Reflection on the Pensive Skill

Fish tanks and think tanks have something in common. They both provide an environment where stopping to reflect is encouraged. It has become necessary in our rapid-paced, quick-action culture to purposely create environments where in-depth analysis can occur. Our pressing social, spiritual, and scientific problems need to be considered more thoroughly than our day-to-day culture allows.

All of us need the chance, from time to time, to pause and reflect at an in-depth level. We need to reserve the right to stop and analyze before taking precipitous action. When we make this space for ourselves, we can experience ourselves as:

- Prudent
- Strategic
- Wise
- Patient
- "Plan-ful"

This invisible but invaluable activity adds an important dimension of wisdom to our lives. When we take the more *Pensive* approach, we have the personal satisfaction of knowing that taking a bit of time to consider the consequences has made all the difference.

PART TWO

THE EIGHT MAJOR STYLES

FROM SKILL TO STYLE

Assuming that you have taken the time to capture a basic knowledge of the eight primary skills, you will soon discover how helpful this can be for your understanding of the major styles.

The styles are developed by extrapolating the behavior you can expect to see when a particular set of skills are combined. It is something akin to making a stew. If you add onions as an ingredient you will alter the flavor; put in carrots and you produce another. In the same way, the addition of a particular skill to other skills produces predictable behaviors.

Exploring the styles brings you to a point where you can appreciate the information available through *Interpersonal Technology*. It will provide you the basis for developing a strategy for how to interact more effectively with each of the eight styles.

The various skill mixtures result in eight major styles, which are then influenced by the *Active* or *Pensive* skill. The following "tree" will help you see the relationship of skill to style.

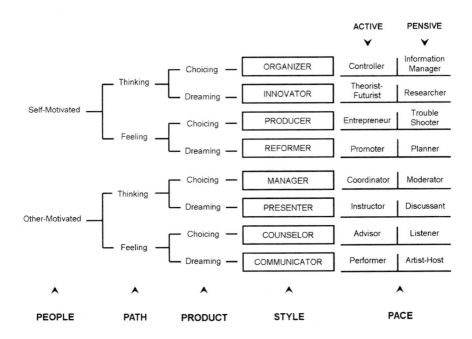

Referring to the tree above, the eight style titles (Organizer, Innovator, etc.) are key words designed to help you remember the style more easily. The second set of words (Controller/Information Manager, Theorist-Futurist/Researcher, etc.) indicates whether the style is expressed more in the *Active* or the *Pensive* mode. Thus, in the first style, the "Organizer" in the *Active* mode would be a "Controller," but in the *Pensive* mode would be an "Information Manager."

If you assessed your own dominant skills as you read the material on the eight primary skills, you can easily trace those skills on the tree above and arrive at your primary style. From there, you can identify whether you take the more *Active* or *Pensive* approach. If you have not already done so, I would suggest you do that now.

As you embark on your exploration of the styles, I hope you find the methodology I have used to present them to be helpful. To make points of comparison readily accessible, I have given a consistent set of information about each of the styles.

First, there is a mythical portrait of someone for each of the eight styles. These eight characters are each composites of a great many people I have known who are of the particular style. As you read these portraits, remember they are designed to give you a general sense of the style.

While creating the portraits, I have put them in the context of an imaginary corporation, the Wonder Works Carpet Company. Each of the eight styles holds a particular position within the company that makes good use of their skills.

In addition to providing these brief portraits designed to give you a descriptive flavor of the styles, I have presented a number of other elements to help you gain an in-depth understanding of each style. These include the following:

> A "tree" tracing the dominant skills in comparison to the other styles
> The dominant driver for each style
> A description of key characteristics of the style
> Non-verbal behaviors indicative of the particular style
> The immaturity factor, describing the misuse of the style strengths
> A basic strategy for working with each of the eight unique styles
> Primary skill combinations for the styles

You will find it helpful to follow the order of the eight styles as they are presented. On the other hand, it is natural to want to read about ourselves first. If you choose to do that, you will have no difficulty in following the descriptions of your style.

You may find it helpful to read the chapter on a particular style and give yourself some time to think about who you know who fits that style, how you currently interact with them, and how this material might suggest some different approaches.

The exploration of styles will help you experience a richness of insight about people and their behavior that can be invaluable to you. We will begin by learning about the first style: the "Organizer."

Chapter 10

INTERPERSONAL TECHNOLOGY

THE FIRST STYLE

THE ORGANIZER

The Organizer

A Brief Portrait

Meet Carl Williams, a forty-five year old vice-president of the manufacturing facility called Wonder Works Carpet. His company produces a national brand of floor covering materials. If you asked Carl how he liked working at WWC, he would not be very revealing. He typically will be more reticent about personal information than he is when discussing something work related. If you asked others in this premier company, they would portray Carl as a serious, hard working, no-nonsense individual. Most of his fellow employees would tell you that they respect him, but that he is difficult to get to know personally.

This particular day, Carl's first challenge involves a management team decision to launch a new line of luxury carpeting that would require a significant change in the production process. It will take considerable convincing for Carl to believe the proposed change makes sense for the company. While Carl will listen to the facts, he often feels that it is his role in the company to be the voice of reason. On several occasions, the "hard questions" he raised caused his peers to rethink an approach they were proposing.

Carl is well aware that others in the organization perceive him as a bit reactionary, or as a guardian of the status-quo, but he doesn't mind that reputation. He feels the role he plays makes an important contribution to the company.

When his point of view does not prevail in a management group decision, he will go along once the decision is reached. As Carl has sometimes said, "Even if the decision is wrong, if we are going to pursue it, my job is to make it work in spite of their wrong-headedness."

What is sometimes amazing to others is that Carl will work diligently for the success of the new decision, while verbally continuing to point out that he thinks the decision may not be the best one. His strong independent thinking will allow him to be comfortable doing this, even when he is making others uncomfortable in the process.

Accuracy is a highly important ingredient in any plan or proposal offered by Carl. Not only is this the case when he is presenting his ideas, it is a cornerstone in his evaluation of others' work. Even if someone has a proposal filled with good ideas, any small errors will frequently cause Carl to mentally discount the value of the proposal. Accuracy is the hallmark of responsibility in

Carl's view. It is a fundamental component in building a sound case. It is a part of Carl's philosophy that accuracy is not merely a matter of having the right concept; it is a measure of your thinking process. Anything less than absolute accuracy down to the last detail is a sign of sloppy thinking.

Other reasons for Carl's success lie in his practice of fundamental management skills, including accurate scheduling, time management, effective cost management, and in-depth product knowledge.

Two areas in which he admittedly has blinds spots are in visioning and taking a creative approach. Still, during the course of his career Carl has developed the maturity to discipline himself to listen, and to be open to ideas that he would not have entertained when he was less experienced.

Similarly, Carl is well aware that interpersonal relationships have not been his strong suit. Earlier in his career he discounted these skills, and it has been costly to him. He is aware of at least one promotion he did not get because he was viewed as less of a "people person" than was desired. At that point he stopped making disparaging remarks about Human Resources and sought the support of that group. As Carl put it, "I wised up and realized that my put-downs were about my discomfort, not about their defects."

At present, Carl is well respected within his company, and is an obvious candidate for the COO position when the person currently in that post retires in two years. His willingness to develop some of the weaker areas in his style has made Carl a viable candidate for the position.

Tracing the Tree: A Path-Finding Process

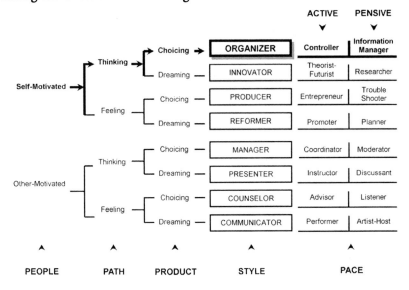

This diagram will help you place the dominant skills of the Organizer style in relation to the other styles.

Skill Dominance

The dominant skills of the Organizer Style are:
Self-Motivated – when engaging in relationships
Thinking – when making decisions or solving problems
Choicing – when implementing tasks

Preferred Pace

The degree of intensity with which the Organizer expresses these three skills will be influenced by the Pace factor: *Active* or *Pensive.*

Active – When Organizers are more *Active,* they are more likely to function in the role of controller. In seminars we sometimes use whimsical characters to demonstrate a point. In the case of the Organizer that figure has been symbolized by a referee, because the Organizer/Controller will tell you when you are "out of bounds." This will take the form of keeping others on schedule, meeting deadlines, and ensuring consistency.

<u>Pensive</u> – When Organizers are more *Pensive,* they can be described as an information manager. They function somewhat like an auditor, tracking and managing by monitoring information or e-mail. If policies and procedures are not in place, they will institute them.

TEN KEY WORDS

Logical	Steady
Reserved	Pragmatic
Thorough	Analytical
Policy Maker	Rule Keeper
Dependable	Detailed

Major Driver: Practical results

Distinguishing Characteristics of the Organizer Style

As we have indicated previously, the combination of Skills produces Style. The following behavioral descriptions will help you recognize the Organizer style. Below, there is an overview for those first wanting the broad perspective, followed by more detailed, in-depth information.

Factual Clarity: Since the Organizer's way of understanding the world is based on a logical assemblage of facts, insistence on clarity is fundamental. Anything that appears to get in the way of a clear path to a logical conclusion will be challenged immediately. Sound reasoning without undue fanfare or unnecessary complication is a highly valued commodity.

Hard sell, strong allies: You will have to prove your case to a person who habitually takes a doubters position in order to ensure sound decisions. Organizers will ask you hard questions; they will be comfortable letting you know they doubt your position, and will expect you to prove its merit. However, if you pass the test of their judgment and they become convinced of the value of your position, they can become strong supporters who have an enduring loyalty. I have come to appreciate this approach of Organizers because it lets me know where I stand. It also lets me know that, once an ally, I can count on them in difficult times.

Sense of Schedule: Organizers often seem uncanny in their ability to predict how long a particular project will take to complete. Their strong connection with practical reality and their logical approach work together to make for good predictors.

Timeliness: Organizers expect professionals to be on time. If you are a more creative type for whom time is less important and you are consistently late, you will be diminished in the Organizer's eyes. There is no reason in their mind for people not to adhere to schedules, and failure to do so will usually be met with a comment about being punctual, or a look that says volumes.

Detail and Accuracy: One of the special gifts that genetics seems to grant to Organizers is the ability to spot errors. It is as if their eyes are drawn directly to the error on page eight of your report. If you have too many simple errors such as typos, it can cause the Organizer to doubt the validity of your ideas. In the same vein, the Organizer wants information in sufficient detail for them to have all the facts. Anything less is not acceptable.

Work and Play: More than any other style, Organizers delineate work and play. Work is work and play is play, and the two do not mix. This explains why they are more serious at work than some of the other styles, and it also explains why they are confused by people who feel it is OK to have fun during the workday.

Rules are Rules: For the Organizer, having a clear set of standards, policies, and guidelines is very important. If these are not in place, they will do what it takes to gain a sense of order and structure.

Guardian of the Status-Quo: Organizers will accept change only after the value of the proposed change has been clearly demonstrated. Otherwise, they will insist that change for change's sake is not a valid reason for altering current practice. Their general sentiment is somewhat akin to the Ogden Nash comment, "Progress might have been alright once, but it has gone on too long."

Practical and Pragmatic: Organizers are quick to tell you that they take the common sense approach. They value the practical way of doing things. They are pragmatic, in the sense that they look for a solution for a particular problem in a particular situation, and when they find a solution, they are quick to use it. They are more inclined to the immediate rather than to looking for long-term solutions that will work in a wide variety of circumstances.

Cost Conscious: Over the years, when I have made proposals for consulting or training, Organizers are the ones who want to know the cost early on. They are not interested in waiting until the end of a proposal to hear information about cost. As managers, they will control expenditures more tightly than any of the other styles. Organizers feel that a financially conservative approach is the wisest course of action.

Organizer Indicators – Detailed Information

Communication Factors: A number of significant things about the Organizer's communication expectations are important for you to know:

- They prefer written information so they can consider it fully before discussing it.
- They practice an economy of words in talking with you. They will generally not elaborate or give details unless asked for them.
- They require highly specific answers to questions and will call your hand on anything less.
- They do not enjoy much social conversation and will generally keep that to a minimum.
- They will not give you many non-verbal signals about what is going on with them. (I will elaborate upon this below in the section on non-verbal behavior.)
- They are put off by an emotional presentation.

Non-Verbal Indicators

The Organizer's non-verbal signals reflect their skill preferences. Recognition of the cues sent by this style can be very helpful aids in your style identification.
Being still while deciding: The *Thinking* skill is engaged when the Organizer moves into the decision-making or problem-solving mode. The result is a decrease in movement. This will take several forms:

- Limited gestures, sometimes limited to the movement of hands and fingers
- Crossing the arms in order to limit movement
- Clasped hands

Lack of facial expression: When engaging in independent thinking, the Organizer often has virtually no expression, or put another way, maintains a fixed expression that gives no signals about their response. This is referred to in non-verbal literature as a "flat affect." This behavior often prompts others to assume the Organizer is being critical or judgmental. When told about this reaction, Organizers are usually surprised, and report that they were only thinking about what they were hearing.

Adopt an independent posture: It is important for Organizers at even an unconscious level to maintain their sense of independence. One of the ways they do so is by refusing synchrony (mirroring of body positions), which indicates connection rather than independence. Thus, if someone comes into their presence and seeks to make connection by mirroring their posture, they will automatically move into a different body position.

Walk/Stance: The *Choicing* skill influences the Organizer's walk and typical stance. As a result, you see some of the following behaviors.

- A crisp walk with the foot hitting the floor heel first. This is related to what can be describe as a "military walk."
- When they stop, the feet will be solidly planted on the floor, with little or no shifting of the feet.
- A stance that is erect, somewhat tense, with arms held close to the body.

Preferring distance: Organizers tend to want a greater amount of physical space than some of the other styles. As an example, they will often move forward to shake hands, and then unconsciously step back slightly to gain that extra little bit of social distance they need.

Voice tone: The Organizer is more inclined to speak in a monotone manner, with emphasis on the end of sentences when they want to make a point. This lowering of inflection is a form of anchoring to emphasize when a choice has been made or a conclusion reached.

Slightly more formal presentation: The seriousness with which Organizers approach work is reflected in the manner in which they present themselves. This includes the following behaviors:

- Fewer smiles
- More serious facial expression
- Fewer verbal interchanges

The Maturity Factor

With each style, there are times when individuals may not express their style in the most mature manner, leading to a misuse of their abilities. This usually occurs when a person overvalues or overuses their preferred skill sets; beyond that, it is also a function of maturity, intelligence, and experience. I have chosen some of the more typical examples of the Organizer's misuse of skills to help you understand the more negative expression of the style.

Overestimate the value of the practical: There is no doubt that one of the major contributions an Organizer makes in the work place is an infusion of common sense and practicality. However, when they refuse even to acknowledge the contribution of creative and innovative input, Organizers can become counterproductive.

Refusal to enter into meaningful discussion: The fierce independence of the Organizer can lead to a refusal to engage in meaningful dialogue with those around them. When this is allowed to happen, both parties lose. This refusal of meaningful dialogue also surfaces in personal relationships. It can be described as stonewalling.

Refusal to decide in a timely manner: Insisting on their own personal timetable for making decisions can result in the Organizer being out of sync with the rest of the organization. Regrettably, they may underestimate the importance of cooperation with others.

Harsh critique: Sometimes Organizers can cross the line with their comments, which often take the form of quick verbal thrusts that can be critical or bitter. These harsh comments are often followed by a refusal to elaborate or explain the comment. They feel the comment should speak for itself.

Long-term sacrifice: The drive for practicality and pragmatism can cause a less-than-mature Organizer to sacrifice long-term interest in lieu of short-term gains.

NON-VERBAL TIPS

The Organizer is turned off by high emotional expression, and will often discount such behavior as weak and unstable. You will get a better reception by exhibiting independence in your interactions. You can maximize your effectiveness with an Organizer by observing the following:

- Do not enter into synchrony too early in the negotiation; lack of synchrony is a test of your strength.
- Limit your movements and gestures, since the Organizer primarily receives information and makes decisions through the Thinking path. Too much movement is distracting.
- Exhibit clear *Choicing* behavior by using downward gestures, and by lowering the inflection on the final syllable in your sentences.

DO'S and DON'TS

Do	Don't
<ul><li>discuss concrete results</li><li>work from a defined policy</li><li>pay attention to bottom line issues</li><li>double check information to be presented</li><li>strive for accuracy</li></ul>	<ul><li>introduce sudden change into a negotiation</li><li>attempt to force a decision too early</li><li>be intimidated by the Organizer's lack of facial expression</li><li>be overly verbal; allow some silences</li><li>be late</li><li>ignore rules, policy, or procedure</li></ul>

SOME WELL KNOWN ORGANIZERS:

Richard Nixon

Bob Dole

Queen Elizabeth

Al Gore

COMMON PROFESSIONS FOR ORGANIZERS:

Accounting

Engineering

Managing Manufacturing Enterprises

THE ORGANIZER

Skill Combinations:

The combination of skills helps us understand style behavior in a fuller and richer manner than is the case when considering the skills separately. The following are some of the key skill combinations of the Organizer style.

Self-Motivated and *Thinking* – This combination makes for a strong sense of comfort with independent thinking. This suggests that the person will naturally prefer thinking through things alone before discussing them with others. They will be very comfortable with their ability to arrive at sound conclusions. Finally, they can take a strong position in the face of differing opinion.

Thinking and *Choicing* – This combination results in a natural tendency to develop logical policies and procedures. Organizers will find it second nature to seek sound, practical approaches when solving problems. They will produce orderly, sequential processes when developing organizational structure. This combination will encourage using vigorous analysis for development of any methods and processes.

Self-Motivated and *Choicing* – This combination of skills makes the Organizer a great defender of the practical approach. They are comfortable challenging new and different ideas, and they feel an obligation to dispute issues based on cost, efficiency, and productivity. This combination may cause them to overlook others' subjective reactions to such a strong pragmatic approach.

Chapter 11

INTERPERSONAL TECHNOLOGY

THE SECOND STYLE

THE INNOVATOR

The Innovator

A Brief Portrait

Some people like to stick to established methods, standard procedures, and well-worn pathways. Paul Albertson is <u>not</u> one of those people. As the manager of research and development for Wonder Works Carpet, Paul's commerce is new ideas, new trends, and finally, competitive new products. For as long as he can remember, Paul has known that he thinks differently than most people. It is clear to him that he is an independent thinker who likes logic and the rational approach, but he is equally clear that he enjoys producing innovative approaches to meet old and new challenges.

In his private assessment, Paul has often thought of himself as a puzzle solver. Give him a problem or puzzle, and his mental processes are immediately stimulated. Moreover, Paul's solutions are not likely to be the most obvious or the easiest approach; instead, they are the most original and groundbreaking.

It would be fair to say that Paul is viewed by his fellow workers as an idea catalyst. He is often the individual who has the new suggestion, the piercing question, or the challenging viewpoint. He is also excited when others present original ideas. For these reasons, Paul is uniquely suited to work with the group who make up the research department.

The employees in the R&D area know that Paul will support their ideas when they are sound, and that he will be scathing in his critique of an idea he considers ill conceived. Importantly, they also know Paul will be a fierce champion of their ideas when it is time to present them for possible application by the company.

Today Paul will be representing the work his department has been involved with for months. The concept, if adopted, will provide the company with a new product using new generation materials that will set a standard for the industry. Paul is aware that there is a lot riding on his presentation in today's meeting. He knows that there will be serious questions about committing the company to such a large undertaking.

One thing that has been pointed out to Paul in the past concerns his presentation methods. Oftentimes, his presentations are overly detailed and ponderous. This has been a difficult behavior for him to alter. For one thing, Paul has a strong belief that people need to understand an issue in a systematic fashion, and that seems to work best by carefully building a logical, step-by-step case. Like many of his friends at the university where he once taught, Paul has an abiding conviction that if he can just get people to understand the facts, they will inevitably have to endorse the idea he is proposing. This belief in *"the power of why"* has often worked against him when he is presenting ideas to people who do not use a framework of sequential, logical thinking.

Paul's relationships within the company are a bit more formal and reserved. He has long been aware that the easygoing camaraderie he sees in other people's interactions does not come naturally for him. While he likes many of his co-workers, his relationships are based more on respect than on emotion. He therefore finds himself gravitating to people who are comfortable exploring ideas. While Paul knows he has the respect of many of his colleagues, he would not go so far as to suggest that he has their affection. Even outside the work setting, Paul is aware that for most of his adult life he has chosen friends on the basis of mutual interest or common ways of thinking.

If given the opportunity to observe Paul's work habits, it would become apparent that in some ways he presents a strange contradiction. For example, while he is open to new ideas and concepts and the change those concepts might suggest, he is much less open to change that involves his personal life or personal habit patterns. When asked to reflect on this, Paul's explanation is insightful. He says, "In many ways my own personal stability is necessary for me to have the kind of environment that allows me to think in a more daring fashion."

Another interesting contradiction centers on his use of ideas. Paul is receptive to ideas and concepts, and is energized by bright new approaches to old problems. Nevertheless, he is much more guarded and defensive about having other people question the soundness of his own ideas. People who deal with Paul have come to recognize that when he has done the work he believes necessary to develop a new concept or theory, he falls in love with that idea. Getting him to reconsider will take significant argument and persuasion.

It is clear that Paul will come prepared to make a very strong case for the new product R&D is proposing for implementation. Not only will he have a strong logical argument, he will provide written documentation to back up the recommendations of his department.

In the meeting today, he will be presenting an idea about which he feels strongly and he will argue forcefully. In other types of meetings, when the group is searching for an idea or addressing a problem, Paul often engages in what can be described as *"negative dreaming."* Before he is willing to consider how something may work to address the problem at hand, he wants to be certain that he has considered all the possible perils and pitfalls that could lead to failure. In exploring those perils, Paul often begins by eliminating approaches that won't work. While this "negative dreaming" behavior may be troublesome and irritating for other members of a problem-solving group, it often serves as a useful and necessary safeguard.

When Paul presents today, it will be from a point of intellectual conviction, based on sound logic and innovative application. After all, he is an Innovator.

UNDERSTANDING THE INNOVATOR STYLE

Tracing the Tree

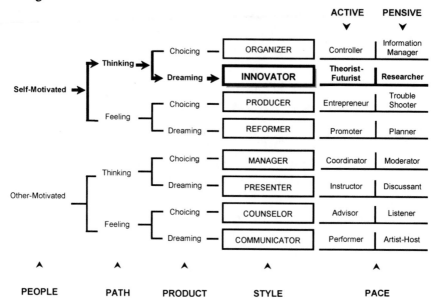

Skill Dominance:

Self-Motivated – when engaging in relationships
Thinking – when decision-making
Dreaming – when implementing tasks

Preferred Pace:

The degree of intensity with which the Innovator expresses these three skill sets will be influenced by the Pace factor: *Active* or *Pensive.*

When in the *Active* mode, Innovators are likely to be more outspoken representatives of ideas and concepts. They enjoy debate and exploration of ideas. Their concepts are often at the leading edge, and will include a futuristic element.

When operating in a *Pensive* mode, Innovators tend to pursue their ideas in a more private manner. The *Pensive* Innovator will be more the researcher and writer, less inclined to public presentation or debate.

TEN KEY WORDS

Abstract	Inventive
Reserved	Strong Opinion
Futuristic	Analytical
Unorthodox	Data Oriented
Stable	Researcher

Major Driver: Idea Catalysts

Distinguishing Characteristics of the Innovator Style

The following are some of the most common behaviors exhibited by this style:

Idea Catalyst: Innovators often feel that one of the things they do best is to promote ideas and to prompt ideas from others.

The Road Less Traveled: This style is comfortable taking the unorthodox approach when it appears to lead to a new truth. This characteristic of intellectual independence can become a point of personal pride.

Keeping Their Distance: Innovators are more reserved and formal than most people. They acknowledge that making "small talk" is difficult for them. As a result, they will often seek out acquaintances that provide mental stimulation and challenge, rather than look for close buddies.

Devil's Advocate: It will be natural for the Innovator to challenge another person's logic. Innovators are willing to play the role of devil's advocate in order to encourage debate. Assuming this role is sometimes misunderstood by others, and is interpreted as being unnecessarily uncooperative. When playing this role, Innovators may ask challenging and provocative questions if they feel that is necessary to get the facts on the table.

The Power of an Idea: It is clear that Innovators believe ideas are the prime movers that produce action. They are the most pleased when they have developed an original idea that has the potential to make significant impact.

Problems as Puzzles: Innovators love mental challenges, and many of them say that they view a problem as a puzzle to be solved. They are readily challenged and become strongly engaged in addressing unsolved problems. When solving problems they will, if given the opportunity, develop multiple options before settling on one. Their natural tendency is to explore potentialities and possibilities.

Deadlines versus Outcomes: This style is more concerned with the quality of the end product than with meeting a deadline. Therefore, they may at times ignore deadlines in order to produce a superior result. Their sense of independence allows them to take this action even when others may be critical of them.

Negative Dreaming: When Innovators are part of a problem-solving group, they often play the role of ensuring that all contingencies are considered. They do this to make certain the group considers all the possible ways a potential solution may go wrong before they select a course of action. While this behavior is sometimes misunderstood and viewed as unnecessarily negative, it is a valuable contribution. It can help the group avoid decisions that result in unintended consequences.

Home-Base Stability: Innovators often take positions that can be both unorthodox and controversial. However, in their personal environment, they are likely to seek stability and consistency. They tend to report that a stable environment is very important to them. While they may theoretically recommend change, they do not thrive on change in their personal lives. Innovators need a secure platform from which to launch their more revolutionary ideas. If the personal environment is chaotic, that takes energy away from their primary goal of being a mental catalyst to others.

As a general rule, this style will work best in an environment that is quiet and private. Too much interaction interrupts their analytical thinking process.

Thinking Time: Their intellectual independence causes Innovators to trust their logic more than most people. As a result, they prefer to think things through first, and discuss them with others after they have reached their own conclusions.

Non-Verbal Indicators

Innovators' non-verbal behavior is tied to the dominant skill preferences of their style. Their non-verbal behavior reinforces these preferences in three areas:

1. There are non-verbal behaviors that help the Innovator maintain an optimum environment for analytical processing.
2. There are behaviors that create and maintain personal comfort.
3. There are behaviors that encourage the exploration of ideas.

We will explore each of these separately to help you develop your ability to recognize this style.

Area One: Maintaining an Optimum Environment for Analytical Processing

Flat Facial Expression: Innovators often listen to others' conversation with an impassive expression that gives little clue as to what they are thinking or feeling. This can be quite intimidating to the other person, since they are getting no feedback as to how the Innovator is receiving their information. There is a natural tendency to assume that no response is a negative response, and to decide that the person is either disagreeing or being judgmental. In actuality, for the Innovator, this inexpressiveness allows them to focus on their internal thinking process, rather than expend energy through facial responses. This is not a conscious choice, but is a natural response when they are listening to information worthy of consideration.

Refusal of Eye Contact: The Innovator may refuse eye contact while listening to you. Instead, they may focus on a spot on the floor or wall in order to limit visual stimulation. The intent is to stay internally focused, rather than splitting focus and reducing their amount of internal processing.

Folded or Crossed Arms: As mentioned earlier in our discussion of skills, folded arms is generally defined as a sign of resistance in our culture. In reality, for some people it may signify just the opposite. Again, this is a limitation of movement that helps the person stay internally focused; it helps them create an environment for analyzing what you have to say. Rather than being resistant, it means they are taking your words extremely seriously!

Long Pauses: The Innovator will feel free to allow long pauses while they think through what you have said. The pauses do not feel unduly long to them, since they are engaging in a sequential process of analysis. To the other person, however, the pause may feel much longer. In conjunction with the impassive expression described above, these two behaviors can be really uncomfortable for others. This is especially true if we are not aware that internal processing is occurring.

Unexplained Smile: There are times when Innovators see nothing of interest going on around them, and they "go inside and have an internal dialogue." They are often exploring a concept when they do this. If they happen to come to an unexpected conclusion, they may register their mental surprise with a slight smile. To observers, it is an unexpected smile, since it has nothing to do with what is occurring externally. The Innovator will rarely provide an explanation.

Area Two: Creating Personal Comfort

Social Distance: The Innovator will normally maintain a greater degree of social distance than people in the general population. The informal social rule when relating to them is, "Not too close, thank you." If you break that rule, they will let you know by disapproval signals or by physically backing away.

Facial Expression: Not changing expression while listening and analyzing is common, but they may use a disapproving facial expression to register disagreement. This may occur while you are speaking directly to the person, or when they are part of an audience. It allows them to register a difference without engaging in a discussion they may not wish to enter.

Hello is Enough: Innovators generally would prefer not to shake hands as a form of greeting, but in a position where they must shake hands, they will usually extend their arm straight out in order to maintain as much distance as possible between themselves and the other person. I sometimes compare this behavior to a stiff arm in football.

Who Cares: In many cases, Innovators have little regard for outward appearance, since it is internal ideas or the life of the mind that is truly important. Social convention takes a back seat to personal preference.

Area 3: Encouraging the Exploration of Ideas

Animation: When Innovators have an exciting idea, they may suddenly become animated and stimulated. The contrast with their usually more restrained behavior is seen by others as dramatic.

Floating Gate: The last thing the Innovator wants is to be earthbound, to be stuck in repetitive thinking. Upward movement reflects this desire to take flight, so to speak. When in a more _Dreaming_ mode, the Innovator often will walk on the front portion of the foot. It may almost be described as a shuffle. There is less tendency to lift the foot, and more tendency to slide it forward.

Upward Gestures and Glances: As is the case with the Innovator's walk, upward gestures and upward glances encourage the expression of the _Dreaming_ skill. These behaviors will become more pronounced when the Innovator is exploring or explaining a new idea.

Favorite Places: The Innovator may become very attached to familiar places, seating, and the like, as part of claiming a place to create. They may resist anything that would require them to change those preferences.

The Maturity Factor

The most prevalent problem area that occurs with the Innovator style is due to the maturity factor. In this case, they may fail to develop the insight that allows individuals to interact with others in a positive and constructive manner. The following list will highlight the most common spheres in which the Innovator style encounters difficulty.

Implied Superiority: There is a tendency for less mature Innovators to assume that, because they are logical and take a more intellectual approach to many matters, they are in fact superior. Unfortunately, Innovators are often unaware that they are conveying this attitude non-verbally. It is a form of elitism that produces a very negative response in others.

Intellectual Impatience: Since the Innovator style is very comfortable with abstract thinking and conceptualization, there is a tendency to become impatient with those who do not move through mental calculations as quickly. They make this known through gestures of impatience or annoyance. It can create significant resentment in others.

Second Guessing: The tendency to always think one has a better idea or a more refined view can lead to considerable second-guessing of others' plans, approaches, or actions. When carried to extremes, this becomes a point for conflict.

Abrasive Behavior: Innovators' self-confidence in knowing they have a good idea can encourage them to express their opinions assertively, but when there is a lack of self-awareness, they can move beyond assertive expression and become abrasive.

Idea Isolation: There is a tendency among some Innovators to relate with their ideas so strongly that they withdraw from personal contact. Good ideas that remain in a vacuum provide little opportunity for corporate or community benefit. The question for the overly reflective Innovator is, "How far is too far away from others?"

Theoretical versus Practical: Being unwilling to see the value of a practical approach, or labeling such approaches as crude or simplistic, can create a chasm that is destructive for Innovators.

Strategies for Working with the Innovator:

Innovators respond best to adequate background and orientation concerning the issue at hand. They appreciate sound logic and unemotional presentations. Most individuals of this style believe that if a person can understand the <u>why</u> concerning an issue, he or she will be persuaded to agree. Another important hint is that the Innovator has a natural tendency to play "devil's advocate" in order to see how well you can present your position. The Innovator delights in new ideas, new approaches, and new concepts. Your best chance for a positive outcome will occur if you can present your ideas in a logical but inventive framework.

NON-VERBAL TIPS

The Innovator approaches negotiations with strong opinions, but with an outward sense of reserve, and it will be important for you to maintain a reserved attitude as well. This includes not moving too close within the person's body space, and not exhibiting too much activity through hand gestures or body movement.

Present yourself in a manner that suggests quiet competence. This non-verbal statement should include an understated non-synchrony.

During negotiation, or when discussing a new approach or concept, use upward gestures to convey your willingness to explore options.

DO'S and DON'TS

Do	Don't
• stay away from "either/or" stances • challenge ideas carefully and respectfully • provide privacy • give a history of the situation • focus on potential • reinforce the Innovator's ideas • present open-ended problems	• squelch the Innovator's dream or concept • leap to the conclusion that early positions are firm positions • be in a hurry to reach conclusions • create conflict for the sake of power statements

SOME WELL KNOWN INNOVATORS:

Jimmy Carter

Albert Einstein

COMMON PROFESSIONS FOR INNOVATORS:

Engineering

Academic

Research & Development

THE INNOVATOR

Skill Combinations:

The combination of skills helps us understand style behavior in a fuller and richer manner than is the case when we consider them individually. The following are some of the key combinations of the Innovator style.

Self-Motivated and *Thinking* – This combination results in the Innovator being very much an independent thinker. They are not unduly influenced by peer pressure, and do not readily alter their beliefs. These combined skills also encourage trust in logical methodology, and stress the importance of self-knowledge.

Thinking and *Dreaming* – This skill combination produces a strong appreciation for originality. It is natural for the Innovator to expand an original discovery into a comprehensive theory by exploring alternate options. This combination also insists on the use of logic as the primary measuring stick when evaluating a new concept.

Self-Motivated and *Dreaming* – The Innovator is the vanguard of new concepts or theories. This combination of independence and identification with creative ideas means the Innovator will be willing to defend a new concept even in the face of strong opposition.

Chapter 12

INTERPERSONAL TECHNOLOGY

THE THIRD STYLE

THE PRODUCER

The Producer

A Brief Portrait

Mary Burns has moved up rapidly to her current position as Wonder Works Carpet's Senior Vice-President of sales. Everyone who knows Mary recognizes that her success has been directly attributable to her level of performance. Beginning as a salesperson, she was promoted to sales supervisor, then to district manager, regional manager, and now to her present position. In every one of these jobs, Mary has had the same motto: "Make good things happen." Her results-oriented approach established her reputation as a "can-do" person early on in her career.

The way Mary sees it she has two major challenges. The first is managing the sales force, and the other is the external competition. If she can be successful with these two major areas, she knows she will succeed personally.

Mary is aware that managing the sales force is a different challenge than the ones she met earlier in her career. Before, she could be successful primarily through her individual efforts. Now that she has responsibility for the entire Wonder Works sales force, her success depends upon getting results through others.

She has adjusted to this challenge by using some of her most trusted skills. To make things happen through others, her approach has been to take a strong leadership stance. In Mary's estimation, there is no substitute for personally championing the cause she represents. When WWC is launching a new product, she is highly visible and verbal.

Mary feels she is well equipped to deal with the second major challenge – that of besting the external competition. One of her natural assets is a keen spirit of competitiveness. She likes the heat of competition and is energized by a challenge. Far from being intimidated when a rival company launches a sales campaign, Mary responds with her own brand of counter-offensive. In these periods of challenge, Mary envisions herself as a general who sounds the call to action and ensures that momentum is maintained.

Her need to move into action is very high, so delays caused by slow decision-making really bother Mary. A phrase that has become a trademark for her is, "cut to the chase." It is a shorthand way to remind others that they had better move to a conclusion pretty quickly.

When in her decision-making mode, Mary is comfortable having someone give her the bottom-line statement about a situation, and then allowing her to ask the questions she needs to feel comfortable with a decision.

Mary often has an intuitive sense of what ought to be done based upon her past experience, and her ability to follow her instincts has paid off over the years. Being able to decide quickly and move rapidly into action has enabled her to get the jump on the competition.

This strong action-orientation has put Mary in conflict with other more careful and constrained colleagues from time to time. Right now, she knows that her relationship with Paul Albertson, who manages research and development, is a bit strained. A few months ago, Mary confronted Paul about taking too long in the research phase, not bringing a product to market when it would have placed them well ahead of the competition. To some degree, she sees it as part of her job to keep R&D on a realistic pace. At least she has a strong supporter in Jerry Delaney, her counterpart in marketing. They share a sense of the importance of getting a product on the market as quickly as possible.

In addition to the alliance with Jerry Delaney (Reformer style), the key relationship Mary believes is crucial to her success is with Carl from manufacturing (Organizer style). She continues to work closely with him, keeping the lines of communication open by appealing to Carl's sense of practicality and his need to see results.

Another key to Mary's success is her willingness to take risks. On any number of occasions, the commitment she made to a project entailed a distinct element of risk. While she is conscious of risks, Mary is not intimidated by them. That has allowed her to move into action while others hesitated. Her strong practical viewpoint gives her the confidence to believe that the course she is pursuing is the right one.

Although this strong sense of practicality is a source of confidence that allows Mary to operate with personal assurance, it has also served as a guard against taking foolish risks. As Mary recently put it to one of her colleagues, "I take informed risks based on common-sense practicality, not foolish risks based on blind emotion."

Mary is a woman of independence, which comes through in the way she exercises power. Much of that power is signaled through non-verbal behaviors such as a claiming of space, a strong voice, and a firm handshake. Whatever its form, the non-verbal message is consistent; it says, "Here is a person who intends to make impact."

UNDERSTANDING THE PRODUCER STYLE

Tracing the Tree

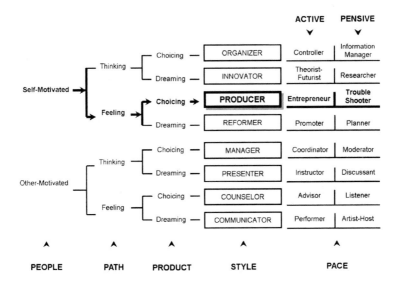

					ACTIVE	PENSIVE
					∨	∨
	Thinking	Choicing —	ORGANIZER		Controller	Information Manager
		Dreaming —	INNOVATOR		Theorist-Futurist	Researcher
Self-Motivated →		Choicing →	**PRODUCER**		Entrepreneur	Trouble Shooter
	Feeling	Dreaming —	REFORMER		Promoter	Planner
	Thinking	Choicing —	MANAGER		Coordinator	Moderator
		Dreaming —	PRESENTER		Instructor	Discussant
Other-Motivated		Choicing —	COUNSELOR		Advisor	Listener
	Feeling	Dreaming —	COMMUNICATOR		Performer	Artist-Host

PEOPLE   PATH   PRODUCT   STYLE   PACE

Skill Dominance

Self-Motivated – Possesses a sense of self-assurance and is comfortable expressing independence

Feeling – Global decision maker who utilizes intuition

Choicing – Wants practical results and makes choices to support a practical outcome

Preferred Pace: The degree of intensity with which the Producer expresses each of the three skills above will be influenced by the Pace factor: *Active* or *Pensive.*

When the preferred pace is to be more *Active,* Producers will be much more action oriented than other styles. The strong need to make things happen motivates Producers to become very directive and assertive in their call to action.

When their preference is the *Pensive* mode, Producers often move into the role of questioner. They will use their reflective ability to achieve meaningful solutions to problems. Even with a *Pensive* pace, the Producer is oriented toward developing a strategy that will lead to action.

TEN KEY WORDS

Action	Response
Results	Outspoken
Direct	Challenger
Entrepreneur	In Charge
Trouble Shooter	Decision Maker

Major Driver: Producers can be aptly described as "action catalysts." Taking action or directing others to do so is second nature for them.

Distinguishing Characteristics of the Producer Style

Rapid Response: Their strong sense of independence makes it easier for Producers to insist on an immediate response. If they sense a lack of appropriate action, they will not hesitate to be more direct in their request.

Timeline: Since the Producer is more action oriented than other styles, the predominant timeframe is now. If you promise to do something for this person, you had better be prepared to act on your commitment or to answer for why you have not!

Verbal: Producers enjoy making impact, and one of the most direct ways to do that is through verbal expression. An obvious example is that they prefer to discuss issues verbally rather than using written communication.

If you bring Producers written information that contains lots of detail, they will likely ask for a verbal overview. They will review details when necessary, but an oral summary is their preferred channel of communication.

Global Thinkers: Producers' approach to making decisions and solving problems is strongly tied to utilizing their experience base. Getting a sense of the situation, mentally comparing it to similar ones, and developing a potential solution is their preferred approach. This style will resort to a more detailed logic process only when it appears that no other method will work.

Pragmatist: When faced with a challenge, the Producer will not be bound by heritage or tradition. If a solution appears to be workable, they are ready to act on it even if it is not the way things have been done before. For Producers, the goal is not to find a solution to a problem that will work in <u>all</u> cases, but to find one that will work <u>this</u> time. They will show little patience with someone who wants to consider theoretical options once a viable solution is at hand. As one Producer put it, "Why dally around looking for the perfect solution when you have a perfectly acceptable way to solve the problem?"

Leader: Producers are generally more comfortable in the role of leader than most of the other styles. If there is a leadership vacuum, they will fill it. Their leadership style is based on a strong personal presence, and their ability to make impact is closely tied to their directness.

Involved: Producers feel strongly about any projects or initiatives they lead. They like to stay connected with the action, and are usually more hands-on than some other styles. An image used to illustrate the Producer is that of a movie director. Movie directors cannot simply be concerned with the artistic niceties; they must be in command of an incredible number of factors in movie production. If they lose overall control, costs can quickly skyrocket. In the same way, the Producer thrives on being in touch and in charge.

Power Person: Producers understand power and its function as a key ingredient in effective leadership. Consequently, they are comfortable expressing power, and want you to exhibit sufficient power to appear credible in their eyes. An individual's failure to demonstrate sufficient power will often cause the Producer to lose confidence in the person. If you find yourself dealing with a Producer, don't be surprised to discover that they are testing to see how you react to their power. Responding with a sense of strength and assurance will be a crucial litmus test for you.

Entrepreneur: It will probably come as no surprise to discover that many entrepreneurs fit the Producer style. Their ability to recognize a practical need, to be comfortable with taking risks, and their strong determination to complete tasks are attributes that make for entrepreneurial activity. Their willingness to be strong verbal advocates for projects and to fulfill the role of leader only add to the likelihood of Producers engaging in entrepreneurial enterprises.

Non-Verbal Indicators

Many non-verbal behaviors characteristic of Producers involve expressions of power, or are checks for others' expression of power.

Stance: The Producer has a dominant skill in *Choicing*. One way this skill is expressed is by assuming a very solid stance, with the feet firmly placed and not moving or shifting. They send a message about being practical by being literally down-to-earth with both feet firmly planted. This grounded stance is often in contrast to the upper body, where they may gesture energetically. Such action in the upper portion of the body may give the appearance that they are moving far more than is actually the case.

I experienced this contrast while working with a manager in a one-on-one coaching session to help her prepare for a presentation. As is often the case, I videotaped her practice presentation for the purpose of objective feedback. When I told her before starting the video playback that she had taken a very solid stance and hardly moved her feet, she was quick to disagree. She was certain that she had moved about quite a lot, and was amazed when she viewed the tape. She had used broad gestures, looked from one side of the room to the other, and turned her upper body, but her feet had remained solidly planted during the entire presentation.

This mixture of taking a solid stance combined with considerable expressiveness in the upper body is common for Producers.

Stance and Territory: At times, stance is also used to make a statement about authority. This is done by placing the feet wider apart and pointing the toes out slightly, making the stance a very wide "V." The non-verbal message conveyed is akin to entering a room and announcing how much of the territory we claim. By according oneself an especially wide "slice of the room," we send a message about confidence and territorial claim.

Tone and Volume: Both tone and volume can be used to send messages about the exercise of power. This is seen with Producers when they raise their voice volume to make a point. They may also give emphasis by lowering voice inflection on words they feel are important. The firm expression of a word uttered in a lower tone is almost like hitting a gavel to make a point. Coupled with raised volume, this lowered inflection conveys a distinct message of authority.

Impact Smiles: When interacting with others the Producer will often present a broad smile. This is not the affiliative "response smile" exhibited by more relationship-oriented people in reaction to a smile from another person. Rather, the impact smile is expressed in order to make a positive impression.

When Producers want to make a positive impact, they may enter the room with a broad smile. It is one part of a very powerful visual and verbal presentation made by the Producer as an influencer.

Eye Contact: Producers often use eye contact in two contradictory ways. First, they utilize wide visual scanning. They will enter a room and make eye contact with others all around the room in a manner that announces their presence. In contrast, sometimes they may refuse eye contact altogether in order to express independence or to test another's resolve. This refusal of eye contact may be in the form of continuing to look at something they are reading and expecting you to press your conversation anyway. Nowadays, it is also likely to take the form of staring at the computer screen and not turning around when another person enters the room to initiate conversation.

Proximity: Another way to express authority and power is through claiming space with the body. When making impact, Producers will often move in very close to another person, speak in a strong voice, and give direct eye contact. Using the body to move into someone's comfort zone of personal space makes the Producer's presence known in a way that is hard to ignore. It is also a means of testing another person's resolve when confronted. If the other person pulls away or exhibits significant discomfort, it signals to Producers that the other person is uncomfortable with their expression of power.

If the person backs away, the Producer may followed this by a whole series of moves to test at what point the person can be comfortable with intrusion. This is not simply a matter of the Producer expressing power; it is a means of determining how much personal power the other person feels. Since Producers like to express power, they are most comfortable with others who can do so as well.

Forceful Gestures: Producers commonly employ forceful gestures to reinforce their strong belief in a course of action. Such gestures include a percussive hand-chop done in mid-air, pointing a finger directly at another person, or snapping the wrist with a closed fist. They will also include broader gestures that extend the arms well beyond the front of the body. These gestures are expressed with energy. They are abrupt and pronounced in order to make emphasis.

Non-synchronous: The Producer, more than any other style, will actively express independence through non-verbal means. This will include a natural tendency to assume body postures that signal independence. If you are talking with a Producer and lean forward in conversation, it is unlikely that the Producer will become synchronous and lean forward with you. This refusal of synchrony is not so much an indication of disagreement as it is a statement of independence.

Anchoring: Producers will use anchoring to make a point or to reinforce a behavior they want from another person. Anchoring includes behaviors such as slapping the knee or thigh at a point of emphasis, lightly slapping or tapping the table, chopping one hand into the palm of the other, or forcefully numbering points as they make them by ticking them off on the fingers. All these actions reinforce or emphasize the Producer's directive or persuasive behavior.

Rapid Response Patterns: It is not only <u>what</u> you say to a Producer that makes for effective communication, it is <u>how</u> you say it. Producers express themselves through quick responses to questions and comments, and they expect a rapid response from you. They often see taking time for reflection before answering as indecisiveness. (Likewise, others sometimes view Producers as firing off a comment so quickly that it is disconcerting.)

Walk: Producers, with their preferred skills of *Feeling* and *Choicing*, will be both energetic and percussive in their walk. They will walk across the floor in a pronounced manner, hitting the heels on the surface with much more percussion than do most people. In males, this often takes the form of a broad stride and swinging arms that exude energy and certainty. In females, the stride may be less pronounced, but they express great energy and intensity through very firm striking of the heel when walking. This is the woman whose staccato click of high heels can be heard from far down the hallway.

Handshake: The handshake of the Producer is very firm. In men, this is the "bone crusher" who makes you wish you were not wearing a ring. In women, it may simply be a much firmer grip than usual. In both males and females, Producers tend to extend their hand forcefully enough to push your arm back toward your body. This push of the hand in your direction is a subtle movement into your personal territory. In its strongest from, the Producer's handshake is one that will drive the other person's hand back until it almost touches their belt. In this case, the hand is driven virtually into the body. This assertive handshake is accomplished so rapidly it is often something of a surprise to the other person.

The Maturity Factor

As we saw in the earlier chapters, all of the skills are vulnerable when used inappropriately or taken to the extreme. There are also some <u>combinations</u> of skills that are likewise vulnerable. In the case of the Producer, the combination of the *Self-Motivated* and *Feeling* skills can sometimes lead to a false sense of certainty. The other dangerous combination for Producers is that of the *Self-Motivated* and *Choicing* skills, which can result in low tolerance for ideas that are not practical and that are not their own. The following are some specific examples of behaviors that can occur when the Producer's dominant skills are misapplied.

Impulsivity: For Producers, this is perhaps the most visible and most frequently noted over-expression of skills, since the repercussions frequently affect other people. Impulsivity occurs when the person ignores important information and relies solely on personal experience as the basis for making a decision. This can be a particular problem with those who have a poor or limited experience base. Conversely, it also occurs in Producers who allow strong emotions and the heat of the moment to outweigh prudent use of their ample past experience.

Verbally Dominant: When challenged, Producers may misuse their sense of independence and their high level of feeling by becoming verbally dominant. This may include raising the voice, anchoring words more strongly, or simply expressing strong emotion to the point of being intimidating to others. One of the real dangers of this behavior is that it may be so threatening to others that they stop sharing important information lest it upset the Producer.

Risk Prone: The high level of self-confidence Producers experience can lead them to take undue risks. When operating within a productive range, Producers' confidence makes them effective leaders because it allows them to take appropriate risks with greater comfort than most people. However, when legitimate self-assurance is inflated to a point of taking unnecessary risks, the results are often adverse. In many cases, over-risking exacts costs in terms of time, money, and the efforts of others.

Competitive: A healthy sense of competition has been a valued trait in American culture. When taken to an extreme however, this trait moves into the realm of being overly combative. When competitiveness becomes excessive, consequences are ignored in the pursuit of winning. There are times when winning at all costs is simply too costly. Producers who become overly aggressive run the risk of losing even while they win.

Feelings Over Facts: Producers have an uncanny knack for using global thinking to arrive at conclusions. When engaging in this kind of intuitive decision-making, they reach conclusions much more rapidly than those who use more traditional logic. This skill enables Producers to move into action before others. Because getting this head start is so valuable to the results-oriented Producer, they will have a tendency to go with their feeling, when taking a more measured approach would have a better outcome.

Cultivating "Yes" Men or Women: A misuse of confident leader skills occurs when the person assembles a group of people whose only job is to carry out the wishes of the leader. In these situations, expressions of empowerment are seen as insubordination. The unfortunate result in work settings is the development of a very weak management team in contrast to the very strong leader. In a family setting, this is illustrated by a quotation I recall: "Father is always right; inaccurate and uninformed sometimes, but <u>always</u> right."

Strategies for Working with the Producer

The Producer likes to produce <u>results</u>. This person is an action catalyst and has a high need for accomplishment. You will need to keep in mind that they will sometimes make dramatic proposals in order to move through detail and achieve a goal. This means you must be ready to make rapid and firm responses to their strong proposals.

Producers are pragmatic, practical, and solution-oriented. Their concern for solving the problem at hand may receive much more attention than the long-term implications. At home or at work, the Producer's tendency is to <u>fix</u> problems as they arise.

NON-VERBAL TIPS

The Producer's tendency to make bold non-verbal statements offers an interesting interpersonal challenge. You will need to show an equal amount of strength without becoming overly competitive. This can be accomplished in several ways:

- Make sure not to back away when the Producer moves into your space.
- Take independent postures and maintain them in the face of challenge.
- Use numerous downward gestures and inflection.

DO'S and DON'TS

Do	Don't
• Mix it up – Producers like a strong interchange • Ask for reactions – Producers usually know what they feel • Look for ways to anticipate their actions • Respond verbally • Offer concrete solutions • Bend the rules when possible for the sake of resolution • Be specific	• Give too many details • "Yes, but…." It invites arguments • Attempt to overpower a Producer – you'll lose. • Become impulsive • Patronize them • Be intimidated

SOME WELL KNOWN PRODUCERS:

Lyndon Johnson

Madeline Albright

George W. Bush

COMMON PROFESSIONS FOR PRODUCERS:

Entrepreneur (new business)

Attorney (trial lawyer)

Positions of Authority

THE PRODUCER

Skill Combinations:

Self-Motivated and *Feeling* – Their self-confidence, coupled with making decisions relying on their experience base, equips Producers to take action more comfortably than others.

Feeling and *Choicing* – A natural consequence of this skill combination is practical solutions decided upon through global thinking.

Self-Motivated and *Choicing* – This combination generates a strong results-oriented set of behaviors. The Producer is driven to make practical choices and to follow through on the choices as decisively as possible.

Chapter 13

INTERPERSONAL TECHNOLOGY

THE THIRD STYLE

THE REFORMER

The Reformer

A Brief Portrait

Jerry Delaney has been director of marketing for Wonder Works Carpet for the past three years. Unlike most people in the organization, Jerry did not move up through the ranks of the company. Before coming to WWC, he had been director of marketing for a major construction company, and prior to that held marketing positions in a food service company and an auto dealership. It has always felt natural to Jerry to look for opportunities to move up. If that has meant moving out of one company and into another, he has been perfectly willing to do so. In fact, Jerry is well aware that he will probably have to move one or two more times to attain the CEO position that is his personal goal.

In Jerry's mind, this does not make him less involved and committed to the success of WWC than some of his colleagues who have been with the company for their entire careers. In fact, Jerry knows his future success depends on making a significant impact in this job, and his personal ambition is strong enough to make him an energetic and committed manager.

One of the things that sets Jerry apart from many of his colleagues is his source of motivation. His motivation is fueled by his internal vision of himself as a leader. He does not need strong organizational identification in order to be committed. He is driven more by his vision of what he wants to accomplish than by mutual identification with a corporate purpose. For the most part, Jerry marches to the sound of his own drummer. It is not that he is a loner – far from it! It is just that he wants people to catch a glimpse of his vision and to join in his causes.

People who watch Jerry in action are sometimes intimidated when he becomes so committed to whatever is his current project. His commitments are not likely to be about ongoing corporate activity, but about the project at hand. He is generally not concerned with routine tasks, and tried-and-true methods hold little interest for him. His excitement is more likely to focus on new concepts, fresh approaches, and exciting campaigns.

More than anyone else on the corporate staff, Jerry is the spokesperson for change. In his estimation, it is clear that marketing drives the business, and that often means selling his peers first. One of Jerry's ongoing challenges has been to convince those who only focus on manufacturing or on keeping the process efficient to look at the bigger picture.

Being on the cutting edge and offering a product that captures the imagination has been a theme he has stressed ever since he arrived on the scene. For many years, WWC was viewed as a high quality but conservative company. One of Jerry's corporate objectives is to help others on the management team recognize the importance of staying ahead of the curve.

A point of puzzlement for Jerry lies in why others don't think in future terms nearly as much as he does. Looking for the obvious future opportunity seems like the most natural thing in the world to Jerry. While others may look for incremental progress through improvement in processes, Jerry's conviction is that the really major gains lie in dramatic departures from the old ways of operating.

However, early in his career Jerry became aware that success was not simply a matter of thinking futuristically and entertaining dramatic departures from past ideas or methods. The other key ingredient in his approach to leadership is being willing to take bold action. One of the gifts inherent in his style has been a strong component of self-confidence. Jerry launches an initiative with supreme confidence that it will be successful. Moreover, Jerry is not inclined to keep his sense of confidence to himself; he conveys it to others. Jerry's best friend has told him more than once that it was not the brilliance of his idea that made a certain project a success, as much as his ability to mobilize others through his infectious self-confidence.

This abundance of confidence has landed Jerry the role of spokesperson on many occasions. Being aware that he can connect with people through public speaking has led him to seek out as many occasions as possible to present. His flair for the dramatic, coupled with his sense of vision, has worked well for him before audiences.

Assuming the role of spokesperson also has it drawbacks. From time to time Jerry raises issues or takes a position that creates conflict. When this happens, Jerry is usually a bit surprised and sometimes suffers momentary emotional hurt. Nevertheless, his strong sense of confidence and underlying independence allow him to bounce back quickly. He will maintain the role of champion of a cause even when that cause becomes controversial. Being the visible and public representative is truly a high for Jerry.

While Jerry does not avoid conflict when it comes as a result of his leadership, he knows that winning others' commitment is more effective than trying to subdue them. One of his trusted tools in working with others is skillfully using the gentle art of persuasion. Jerry can be very persuasive both before an audience or in a one-to-one exchange.

This is one of the reasons Jerry chose marketing as his pathway to personal success. He is not simply good at persuasion; he enjoys the challenge. In fact, this very morning there is a senior management meeting at which he will present a new concept that can put them well ahead of the competition. The R&D group has developed the product, but Jerry believes he has the overall approach that will make it successful.

Even though he knows there will be some strong resistance, Jerry's adrenaline is already flowing. It is time to move ahead!

UNDERSTANDING THE REFORMER STYLE

Tracing the Tree

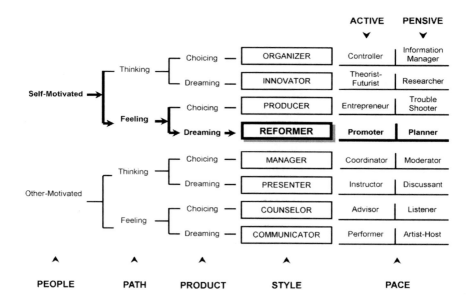

Skill Dominance

The three major skills that combine to produce the Reformer style are:

Self-Motivated – when engaging in relationships
Feeling – when approaching decision-making
Dreaming – when implementing tasks

Preferred Pace

The degree of intensity with which the Reformer expresses these three skills will be influenced by the Pace factor: *Active* or *Pensive.*

When Reformers are more *Active* in preferred pace, they will invest phenomenal amounts of energy in projects or enterprises. They will work very hard to be on the forefront of an issue, and will spend significant energy in the role of pioneer.

When more *Pensive,* Reformers will be inclined toward the role of planner or strategizer. They will utilize their ability to anticipate others' reactions to an issue and will fashion their messages or campaigns to gain maximum advantage. These are often the behind-the-scenes people in political campaigns who know just what spin to put on an issue.

TEN KEY WORDS

Change Agent	Developer
Leader	Visionary
Politician	Advertiser
Pioneer	Enthusiast
Persuasive	Marketer

Major Driver: Serving as the change agent

Distinguishing Characteristics of the Reformer Style

Point of Puzzlement: Since it is so natural for Reformers to think in futuristic, opportunistic terms, they are often puzzled when others don't think that way. They are especially surprised if others view their suggestions as unexpected and outside the norm.

Confidence: Along with the ability to see potential while others may remain mired in detail, it is their self-confidence that allows Reformers to be so comfortable in the role of leader. The result is that Reformers often fulfill the role of spokesperson for their organization. Taking on the role of standard-bearer is not always as glamorous as it may seem, since it often leads to conflict. Newt Gingrich's leadership in the late 1990's U.S. House of Representatives provides a vivid example of this type of confident yet controversial spokesperson.

Risk Prone: Reformers generally have abundant confidence in their enterprises. This confidence leads them to be much more comfortable with risk-taking than the average person. What seems like an extreme risk to others may feel well within the acceptable range of risk for the Reformer. Their ability to take risks where others would hesitate often results in Reformers achieving startling successes. Lee Iacocca's spearheading the rebirth of Chrysler Corporation is an example of a Reformer who is willing to represent a cause and take the necessary risks.

Persuasive: Reformers know that being coerced is not as effective as being convinced. Therefore, they seek to invite people to join a cause. They work to get larger and larger groups to align with the proposed enterprise until they have accomplished their goal. They are so centered on convincing and persuading that they can focus their total energy on that goal.

At SMU, I had the opportunity to work with Claus Rholfs, a classic Reformer. He was invited to SMU with the explicit purpose of launching an intern program to supplement the academic preparation of students in the school of theology. In order to make this happen, our staff of three conceptualized the process. After the initial conceptualization, we were faced with the task of convincing others to come on board.

To many people, the program seemed a radical departure from traditional education. Naturally, a number of these individuals were dubious of the idea. Others were clearly resistant. Claus's approach to winning over the doubters included his own brand of personal persuasion. The result was a presentation planned to inform and enlist others. We made that presentation to over 100 groups across the country. It worked!

Political: In addition to being persuasive, most Reformers are more political in their approach. They sense the value of organizational networks, and they see the value of marketing themselves and their causes. They will use the resources of good public relations, and will make dramatic moves to get their point across. Reformers understand the importance of a symbolic act when they are in the role of standard-bearer, and will be skillful at recognizing symbolic opportunities. Having identified Newt Gingrich as a Reformer, the "Contract with America" serves as a great example of a symbolic act. Choosing that theme, and lining up all those Republican congressional representatives on the steps of the capital to announce the initiative, was classic Reformer symbolism.

Change Equals Possibility: The Reformer's abundant self-confidence and ability to think futuristically results in a belief that any change they envision will be positive. Not only do they believe these changes will be good for themselves, they are certain they will be good for others. Reformers are often able to bring about significant change by the sheer strength of their powerful belief in a cause. On more than one occasion, I have observed effective Reformers convince others to join an effort in the absence of supporting data. People often respond because they are in the presence of the Reformer's powerful conviction. One person expressed this well when discussing a Reformer colleague. He said, "How is it that every time I listen to John tell us about his latest idea, it seems like the best thing since sliced bread?"

Non-Verbal Indicators

Every style has distinguishing characteristics that are most likely to occur with that style. This is particularly true of Reformers since they are so visual and verbal in the ways they present themselves. There is no group more dramatic or skilled at sending non-verbal signals than the Reformer. Recognition of the cues sent by this style can be a very helpful aid for you in style identification.

Facial Animation When Communicating: Reformers are very aware of the impact of non-verbal signals, and will be highly attuned to their audience. Among other signals calculated to influence, Reformers often exhibit a wide variety of facial expressions designed to send their message to the audience. This will be true whether it is an audience of one or an audience of fifty. Unlike with the *Other-Motivated* styles, the Reformer's facial expressions are not in response to signals from others. Rather, they are generated more internally, and are intended to send a message or make an impact.

Broad Dramatic Gestures: The Reformer's *Self-Motivated* and *Feeling* skills result in freedom of expression, including freedom of movement. The Reformer will often use gestures that are suggestive of natural leadership. An example would be outstretched arms lifted above the head, such as we see from the winning candidates at a national political convention. This gesture is an invitation to an audience to respond to the leader. It is interesting to note that media coaches usually train candidates to use classic Reformer non-verbal skills. This is especially important when these are not the candidate's natural behaviors. During the next national political conventions, take note of how long the candidates stand with their arms in a spread-eagle, over-the-head position, and ask yourself just how long that would be comfortable. Better yet, don't wait – just try it for yourself right now and see how long it takes for your arms to fatigue.

Close Proximity: The Reformer's need to make contact and create impact often results in their standing very close to another person when engaging in conversation. This style can easily intrude upon the "ring of comfort" that most people reserve for themselves. Reformers are equally comfortable with you taking similarly close positions.

Power Positions: This style has an innate sense of which chair at a meeting table is the power spot. They sense which positions in a room will afford them the most influence, and will instinctively go to those positions. This may be at the head of the table, or in a position that will afford the greatest eye contact with the designated leader of a meeting. Similarly, Reformers will often make bold changes in position, such as getting up and moving to the opposite side of the room, to indicate they are taking a different position. A classic power gesture can be seen at a meeting table when a Reformer locks both hands behind the head and extends the elbows. This expansive gesture indicates a sense of being in charge and comfortable with the role of leader, and may occur even when the Reformer is not the designated leader for that situation.

Variety of Voice Tones: Just as Reformers will move to a different position within a room in order to dramatically emphasize an opinion, they will also commonly utilize a broad range of voice tones to convey a message. The point of such behavior is to heighten the dramatic effect and to capture the listener's attention. This variety may include differences in volume as well as expressive tones of voice.

Buoyant Walk: Walking on the balls of the feet and striding with a slight spring in the step suggest the Reformer's energy and enthusiasm. Recently I was one of a series of speakers for a conference in which we were all seated on stage and approached the podium when it was our turn to speak. One of the speakers was a Reformer. I was mildly amused to notice that in the midst of his motivational speech, this person literally rose on his toes when standing behind the podium. Even though the audience could not see him standing on tiptoe, he was sending the message that he wanted to rise to new heights and he wanted the audience to join him!

Distinctive Handshake: When Reformers greet you they want to make an impact or connection with you, and their handshake is indicative of this. Generally, Reformers will approach with a smile, extend their hand, take your hand, and pull you in close to them. Quite often they will use their left hand to grasp you at the elbow, or they may turn your arm almost parallel. Once your hand is turned, they will move in very close so that your hand is closely sandwiched between themselves and you. All of these actions are emotionally expressive and invite an emotional response from you.

The Maturity Factor

As has been indicated for each style, there are times when individuals may not express their style in the most mature manner, leading to a misuse of their assets. This is most likely to happen with Reformers when they have extended themselves beyond their limits of endurance.

It can be said of Reformers in general that they will throw themselves into a new initiative with a wholeheartedness that often intimidates others. The result is that they will sometimes extend themselves to the point of becoming emotionally and mentally depleted. When they reach this point, Reformers may attempt to shortcut important processes in order to reach their desired goal. In these cases, they are likely to manifest one, several, or even all six of the behaviors described below.

Illusions of Grandeur: Once in the *Dreaming* mode, it is only a short step from having a sense of vision to starting to believe that vision has already become reality. The result can be an illusion of grandeur resulting in actions and decisions based on the desired vision, rather than on present reality.

Refusal to Face Facts: When on overload, Reformers' desire to achieve a goal may result in them becoming much less open to information that would contradict the scenario they have already constructed. The very strong ego of many Reformers will enable them to shut off new or distracting information that could disrupt a desired course of action.

Ideas, Ideas, Ideas: One of the ways the Reformer may meet a crisis is by producing creative ideas. When operating in a positive and constructive range, this is one of the Reformer's major assets. When they move into a more reactive or high-stress mode however, Reformers may begin to suggest so many ideas that the sheer overload created can bring down an organization.

I recall the head of an organization who sought to meet a crisis by generating a nightly list of ideas for the company to undertake. He was saved from becoming destructive by a strong "number two" person who was able to say, "I know you have 20 good ideas to bring us every morning, but if we try them all we will totally lose our focus. You bring in a list and I will tell you which ones will help us, and which will distract us." Fortunately, the head of the company was able to hear that message and to respond constructively to it.

From Persuasive to Aggressive: When their plans are not coming to fruition and frustration continues to build, Reformers will sometimes cross the line from persuasive to aggressive. This may take the form of more intense political pressure, or it may be direct verbal confrontation. When this type of pressure occurs, it is an over-extension of their positive persuasive abilities.

Tendency toward Mood Swings: Anyone who invests as heavily in a project as a Reformer is likely to be excited when there is success and disappointed when there is failure. Their high-stakes emotional investment makes Reformers far more susceptible to wider mood swings than their more conservative counterparts.

Extreme Insistence on Loyalty: A central element in being persuasive is seeking a sense of commitment from others. One ingredient in the formula for a high degree of involvement is a high degree of commitment, which Reformers expect both of themselves and of others. In times when they are functioning at a burnout level, there is a tendency to demand an even stronger show of allegiance from others. This need for loyalty is a source of reassurance for them about the value of the present cause or concept.

THE REFORMER – RECAP

Reformers are involved in either direct or indirect persuasion almost continuously. Negotiation, therefore, is approached by this style more as a matter of persuasion than a logical process. They enjoy visualizing possibilities and convincing others of the potential their visions hold. This style usually exhibits considerable wit and charm in dealing with others. However, as persons who invest emotionally in their own concepts, Reformers feel very strongly about their pet projects and may tend to view disagreement as disloyalty or betrayal.

The Reformer generally prefers being the identified leader in new causes and enterprises, and seeks to enlist others in those causes. They like being the pioneers rather than the maintainers.

NON-VERBAL TIPS

Be aware that Reformers often consider emotional expression to be a measure of your positive reaction, and that a lack of affective energy is perceived as a negative response. Thus, be willing to:

- Show your excitement when you agree

- Be energetic in your suggestions and discussions
- Use physical gestures frequently

You may also exhibit the independence the Reformer respects by:

- Maintaining your territory
- Using understated expressions of power when moving in new directions
- Employing upward movements and voice inflections

DO'S and DON'TS

Do	Don't
• make bold proposals • be excited with them • listen to their feelings and not just their ideas • allow them to dream before introducing the practical "how" questions • be ready to move rapidly from topic to topic • look for ways to channel their ideas toward your proposal • be repetitive with your point of view	• become overwhelmed by their forcefulness; remain comfortably firm • be shocked by overstatement or hyperbole • try to calm them down; channel their energy instead • disagree about small details, but do stand firm on big issues • withdraw • be overly sensitive

REMEMBER: Reformers will be much more receptive to your detailed proposal if you can work out a broad plan that will fit their conceptual framework.

SOME WELL KNOWN REFORMERS:

Bill Clinton

John F. Kennedy

Oprah Winfrey

Tom Peters

Norman Schwarzkopf

COMMON PROFESSIONS FOR REFORMERS:

Marketing

Politics

Public Speakers

THE REFORMER

Skill Combinations:

Self-Motivated and *Feeling:* This combination particularly influences the manner in which the Reformer relates to others. Due to the combination of these two skills, Reformers will present themselves to others with an air of confidence and emotion that can be highly persuasive.

Feeling and *Dreaming:* The *Feeling/Dreaming* combination encourages Reformers to produce many ideas that they are likely to feel strongly about. This combination also allows Reformers to present new ideas with a high degree of energy and excitement. Even when they are more *Pensive,* they will want the wording and the form of presentation to have a ring of excitement.

Dreaming and *Self-Motivated:* This combination of skills gives Reformers great confidence in the value of their ideas. It allows them to take a more dramatic or controversial position with more confidence and comfort than most people.

Chapter 14

INTERPERSONAL TECHNOLOGY

THE FIFTH STYLE

THE MANAGER

THE MANAGER

A Brief Portrait

As a member of the senior management team, later this week Wilma Riley will be speaking at the annual corporate communication program. She has been asked to discuss the three work values she considers most important for success at Wonder Works Carpet.

The three values Wilma ultimately selects are not just a matter of theory; they reflect her own approach to work. Her preferences reveal her style.

Wilma has set aside time this morning to decide which three work values she will discuss. In considering her choices, Wilma knows there are numerous values she could choose, but none seems more important than loyalty. As a long time member of the corporate staff, Wilma has a strong sense of personal identity with the company.

Wilma came to WWC shortly after graduating with a degree in business from the state's major university. Her entrance into the company was less than spectacular. She held a series of low-level staff positions, and made relatively little progress for the first five years. This lack of progress, however, was not so much a reflection of Wilma's potential as it was a commentary on the nature of the company twenty-five years ago. At that time, WWC was more of a regional company, with limited growth potential and few opportunities for advancement.

As a result of the obvious lack of opportunities, a number of her less patient contemporaries moved on to other companies early in their careers. Wilma, however, believed that if she stayed with the company her loyalty and involvement would pay off in the long run.

Thinking back on the decisions she made, Wilma realizes that she had a higher degree of trust in the corporate culture than most of her friends. In many ways, that is still the case. Even so, it is hard to argue with experience, and her experience confirms that her loyalty and persistence have paid off handsomely.

Today, when considering the values she believes are important, Wilma is aware that loyalty is a primary measure by which she evaluates her own employees. This is reflected in her expectation that her employees be willing team members.

She is cognizant of the internal Geiger-counter that goes off when she is around some of the high-performance, high-profile newcomers who seem more intent on self-promotion than on working for the good of the company. In Wilma's estimation, being a willing part of the team and working for the overall corporate objective is a major indicator of one's loyalty.

The second major value Wilma chooses to highlight in her speech is being results-oriented. While loyalty and persistence are important, the ultimate proof of the pudding is whether the person can produce concrete results. One of Wilma's personal skills has been her ability to cut through a lot of abstract information and keep a group focused on the job at hand. She is aware of her reputation as a "no-nonsense" manager who gets right to the point when discussing a project with her employees.

This ability to get things done through others has been a particularly important ingredient in Wilma's success. Her range of responsibilities is broad, including new construction, the mailroom, purchasing, travel, and facilities maintenance; success requires that she be able to work effectively through others.

Failure to produce results in any of these areas usually has immediate consequences – none of them good. Therefore, reinforcing the importance of achieving results is more than a value for Wilma; it is a fundamental operating principle. Whenever she is in a meeting, her questions usually focus on what results are being achieved.

The third and final value on Wilma's list is sound preparation. As she thinks about this factor, a frown appears on her face as she recalls a recent incident with one of her key employees. The person came to a meeting obviously not prepared to answer some of the key managers' questions. Wilma had been embarrassed at the lack of professionalism, and was quietly furious with the person. That meeting was followed by a session in which Wilma made it abundantly clear that such an obvious lack of planning and preparation was unacceptable. Her reaction should have come as no surprise to the employee, since one bit of personal scuttlebutt about Wilma is, "You had better have your ducks in a row when you meet with Wilma, or expect to be in trouble."

Always being properly prepared and being on top of issues prevents surprises and increases the chance for success. Being prepared has allowed her to deal with multiple challenges and to continue to get significant results for Wonder Works Carpet.

When she reviews her list and what she will say about each of the three values for success, Wilma is very comfortable with her choices: loyalty, results orientation, and adequate preparation. She will be ready for her presentation on Friday.

UNDERSTANDING THE MANAGER STYLE

Tracing the Tree

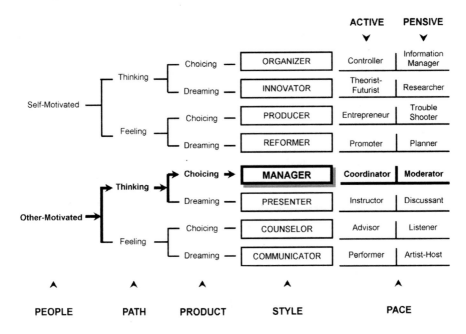

					ACTIVE	PENSIVE
			Choicing —	ORGANIZER	Controller	Information Manager
	Thinking		Dreaming —	INNOVATOR	Theorist-Futurist	Researcher
Self-Motivated			Choicing —	PRODUCER	Entrepreneur	Trouble Shooter
	Feeling		Dreaming —	REFORMER	Promoter	Planner
	Thinking		Choicing →	**MANAGER**	**Coordinator**	**Moderator**
			Dreaming —	PRESENTER	Instructor	Discussant
Other-Motivated →			Choicing —	COUNSELOR	Advisor	Listener
	Feeling		Dreaming —	COMMUNICATOR	Performer	Artist-Host

PEOPLE   PATH   PRODUCT   STYLE   PACE

Skill Dominance

As has been stated previously, all of the eight styles have a set of dominant skills that molds behavior and results in an individual style. The major skills of the Manager are:

Other-Motivated – when engaging in relationships
Thinking – when making decisions
Choicing – when implementing tasks

Preferred Pace

As is the case for all the styles, the Manager's expression of these skills is influenced by the Pace factor – either more *Active* or more *Pensive.*

When Managers are *Active* in preferred Pace, they will be more involved in directing the efforts of others.

When more *Pensive,* the person will be more of a moderator, encouraging the ideas and interactions of others.

TEN KEY WORDS

Patient	Prudent
Logical	Methodical
Coordinator	Consistent
Supportive	Conservative
Team Player	Even

Major Driver: Achieving practical results while being a part of the team

Distinguishing Characteristics of the Manager Style

No Surprises: The Manager style typically likes to plan their work and will expect you to keep them informed about anything that will affect their sphere of activity. Managers often tell employees that they will support their decisions and the actions they take as long as they are kept abreast of what is occurring. On the other hand, if the Manager discovers information from another source, or gets a nasty surprise, this style will feel justified in withdrawing support. A Manager's simple rule might be: "Keep me informed and receive my support; allow me to be surprised and expect my ire."

Seeks and Sustains Stability: The *Other-Motivated* and *Thinking* skills, which are dominant in the Manager style, create a strong need to provide a reasonable and constructive work environment. As a result, Managers strive to provide a work climate where things occur in a structured and orderly manner. They will be on guard against undue interruptions and distractions. While this style will be open to realistic changes, they will resist changes that appear less reasonable or that will create unnecessary chaos.

Coordinator: A distinct competency of the Manager style is the ability to recognize the varied talents and abilities of others and to put those talents to best use.

Team Player: Creating, developing, and sustaining an effective team is a major source of satisfaction for most Managers. Their ability to create a positive structure, to coordinate the various talents in a group, and their stress on loyalty, all encourage team development. If, however, a member of the team shows a lack of cooperation or commitment, the Manager may react by being punitive. Being a team player is something Managers seek to do themselves, and they will have the same strong expectation of others.

Practical Results: The *Thinking-Choicing* skill combination prompts the Manager to seek measurable, reality-based results. When someone promises results that seem overly optimistic or ill founded, the Manager will react with a healthy degree of skepticism.

Reasonableness: Managers like to take a logical approach when discussing issues. They also like to maintain amiable relationships. As a result, this style will often maintain a controlled and understated demeanor even when they may be experiencing strong disagreement internally.

Seeks the Middle Ground: The Manager has a natural aversion to extremes, and thus will often take a more moderate position. This reinforces their belief that they have taken the "common sense" approach.

Present Work is Founded on Prior Preparation: Managers generally want time to "think things through" before reacting. They assume that to do your best job, you need to be prepared. Evidence of a lack of logical preparation will almost surely cause one to lose credibility with the Manager style.

Turns Concepts into Processes: A natural talent for most Managers lies in their ability to turn an idea into a method for getting things done. Managers are usually the ones who want to take the time to develop procedures or devise operating principles. Managers often report that they derive a real sense of satisfaction from helping others make the transition from conceptual to practical in their work environment.

Non-Verbal Indicators

An important thing to remember when using non-verbal indicators to help you identify another person's style is that your best guide is often a *combination* of non-verbal behaviors. Watching for indicators in combination will be a more reliable key in determining someone's primary style.

Fixed Facial Expression While Receiving Information: It is relatively common for the Manager to look almost stern while receiving verbal communication from another. In some cases, this may be misinterpreted as registering disagreement. In reality, it is likely to be simply a limitation of movement in the face while the person is engaged in more left-brain, *Thinking* skill.

Quick Reassurance with Facial Expression: Being more *Other-Motivated* allows Managers to monitor the responses and reactions of others. When they realize that someone is uncomfortable with their fixed facial expression, Managers will temporarily move out of the realm of analytical activity and give a moment of reassurance through a brief smile or a nod of the head.

Limited Gestures: Having a dominant skill in *Thinking*, the Manager will use gestures that are more limited. You will see very few wide sweeps of the hands and arms. Most of their gestures will be in front of the body rather than beyond the body.

Downward Gestures: Managers will often use gestures that suggest closure. These include ticking off the fingers while illustrating points, or softly tapping the table when taking a position.

Lowered Voice Inflection: Another downward indicator is in their use of voice inflection. They will use a lower tone at the end of sentences. Listening for this voice pattern will help you identify that someone is using the *Choicing* skill.

Smooth Walk: The evenness of a Manager's personality is reflected in their walk. Their step often lands in the middle of the foot. You get a sense of a very smooth movement with little bouncing of the head.

Reserve and Restraint in Response to Emotional Behavior: When faced with a high expression of emotionality, Managers often react by sending a non-verbal signal that the person should calm down. The Manager will exhibit a great deal of reserve and restraint in hopes that the other person will get the hint and behave similarly. However, this behavior frequently evokes the opposite reaction, since the emotionally expressive person is often trying to elicit a *more* emotional response from the Manager.

Moderate Synchrony: Managers are most likely to match your body postures and to synchronize movements when they agree with your ideas. They will express more limited synchrony when they disagree.

The Maturity Factor

As is the case with all the styles, Managers do not exhibit an equal degree of behavioral effectiveness. Our differing histories, genetic endowment, opportunities for education, and individual psychological reactions to events, all combine to create our unique manifestation of style.

When the expression of style is less effective, it is often due to using our skills in the extreme. There are six common behaviors that Managers may exhibit when expressing their style ineffectively.

Oversimplification: There is a need to make all things concrete and specific, even at the expense of glossing over or ignoring complex factors.

Repetitive Solutions: They have a proclivity to overvalue practical past experience, and consistently apply past solutions to present problems. This results in the exclusion of more innovative, novel approaches for solving problems. This behavior also leads to discounting the credibility of more unorthodox, creative people.

Misguided Measurements: Loyalty is a highly valued quality in the eyes of the Manager style. However, when undue value is placed on loyalty, there is a tendency to confuse loyalty with productivity. In this instance, the loyalty factor can overshadow actual results.

Misplaced Trust: When a Manager views someone as a solid, loyal member of the work team, he/she will be prone to place an undue amount of faith in that person. They are inclined to assume that person will do the right thing. In cases where this trust is misplaced, it may result in significant harm to the Manager's efforts as well as his/her credibility.

Bureaucratic Shield: Managers move through the organizational maze with more ease than most styles. Therefore, when they feel threatened or become defensive, using the bureaucratic system is a natural and logical tactic for Managers. They are inclined to fall back on a more rigid use of policies, procedures, and directives. For the defensive Manager, the bureaucracy provides a distinct comfort zone.

Change Resistant: In their most effective mode, Managers are good stewards of the systems and processes they manage. They guard against undue disruptions and loss of focus. When less effective, the Manager begins to see suggested changes as a threat. In such situations, they become unduly resistant to change, and have a predisposition toward seeing change agents as the enemy.

THE MANAGER – RECAP

Managers will often describe themselves as practical, team-oriented, and consistent in their approach. They report that they prefer to hear other viewpoints before arriving at a decision, but once Managers have heard the facts, they will often take a strong position. In addition, Managers will often ask others questions in order to make their own point.

Because Managers usually have good social skills, their desire for results and an orderly approach may be somewhat understated. This team leader likes to discuss and solve problems in an orderly manner.

The more analytical Manager will often show very little expression when thinking. However, when they notice others' discomfort, Managers will attempt to offer reassurance with a smile or positive expression.

NON-VERBAL TIPS

When negotiating with the Manager, keep in mind the non-verbal signals involving relationship and decision-making skills. Some positive non-verbal behaviors you may utilize are:

- Show positive response when you receive a positive reaction
- Display limited synchrony
- Do not become overly expressive with gestures or facial expressions
- Use *Choicing* behaviors when discussing possible solutions to deadlocks

DO'S and DON'TS

Do	Don't
<ul><li>Prepare and present your case carefully</li><li>Answer questions as fully as possible</li><li>Look for logical compromises</li><li>Expect a hard line but a tactfully presented negotiation</li><li>Continue to work on differences with patience and persistence</li></ul>	<ul><li>Use the tactic of surprise</li><li>Stray into personal concerns once involved in the negotiation</li><li>Make emotional appeals</li><li>Resort to undue intimidation</li><li>Expect quick responses until the facts are fully understood</li><li>Be surprised at the rapidity of the Manager's call for action once a compromise is reached</li></ul>

SOME WELL KNOWN MANAGERS:

George H.W. Bush

Troy Aikman

Colin Powell

COMMON PROFESSIONS FOR MANAGERS:

Internal Management

Team Leadership

THE MANAGER

Skill Combinations:

In addition to the primary influence of each skill set, the <u>combinations</u> of the dominant skills can help us recognize how a style is developed, and more clearly recognize how it is likely to be acted out. In the case of the Manager, three combinations can help us understand the style a bit more clearly.

Other-Motivated and *Thinking:* This combination particularly influences the manner in which Managers relate to others. When dealing with others, their twin mottos might be:

"Reasonable relationships"
and
"Relationships that make sense"

Thinking and *Choicing:* This combination results in a worldview that suggests: 1) issues should be sense making, and 2) ideas should be related to reality.

Choicing and *Other-Motivated:* Relationships will have a "no nonsense" flavor and should center on achieving results.

Chapter 15

INTERPERSONAL TECHNOLOGY

THE SIXTH STYLE

THE PRESENTER

The Presenter

A Brief Portrait

When Gail Gillespie was in graduate school studying chemistry, it never occurred to her that she would become a senior manager of technical sales for a flooring company. She assumed she would be a teacher, but through a strange set of circumstances, here she is. As it happens, the fit between her natural skills and the requirements of the job are remarkably similar. Wonder Works Carpet sells bonding agents as well as chemicals that protect carpeting and furniture. She loves being in the role of resident expert for the company.

Sometimes Gail's fellow managers tease her about her drive for competence. They gave her a particularly hard time this past summer when she combined her vacation to California with a seminar on a new chemical product that relates to their business. Even she had to admit that might have been a bit much.

However, nobody on the management team complained when she took time to share the information about the new product with them. An operative term for Gail is *important* information. She is genuinely offended when she attends a presentation with lots of fanfare and very little useful information. Consequently, she works very hard to make sure that when she makes a presentation, the information is both informative and relevant.

Gail is aware that she is considered a good presenter. She also knows that the secret to her success is no mystery. As she has explained to employees in her department, it is a combination of two things: solid information and significant preparation. These two factors make her a confident and effective presenter. As she has said many times to people who comment on her presentation style, "There is no substitute for the research that gives you something important to say, and taking the time to prepare to say it well."

Upon reflection, it really is not so strange that Gail is in the position she holds. In many ways, she has in fact become a teacher after all – sharing product information, providing insight about creative applications, and equipping a technical sales force to present their products effectively. All in all, it's a pretty good formula.

UNDERSTANDING THE PRESENTER STYLE

Tracing the Tree

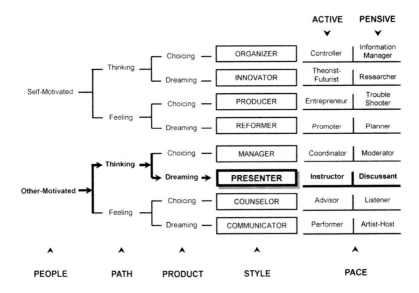

Skill Dominance

The three major skills that combine to produce the Presenter style are:

Other-Motivated – when engaging in relationships
Thinking – when making decisions and problem solving
Dreaming – when exploring potential means of implementation

Preferred Pace

The degree of intensity with which the Presenter relates, decides, and implements, will be influenced by the Pace factor: *Active* or *Pensive.*

When the Presenter's pace is more *Active,* they will be energized to fulfill their sense of vision. Turning their "dreams" into reality is a way of taking a more *Active* approach.

Presenters whose pace is more *Pensive* will be more reflective. They will prefer dialogue over presentation. They will seek to influence through the power of an idea rather than by the intensity of personal persuasion.

TEN KEY WORDS

Instructor	Synthesizer
Balanced	Flexible
Thinker	Social Skill
Future Oriented	Category Builder
Likes Concepts	Reflective

Major Driver: Personal and professional competence

Distinguishing Characteristics of the Presenter Style

Continually seek opportunities for personal development: Presenters' need for competence means they usually participate in formal and informal training. Presenters are often life-long learners, since learning is not only about job effectiveness, but is closely tied to their definitions of themselves.

Open to ideas from other people: The Presenter appreciates a good idea regardless of its source. Building relationships based on shared interests is not uncommon.

Synthesizer of concepts: The Presenter will combine ideas from a variety of sources into an emerging concept. The new concept often goes beyond the original ideas since it is based on the implications of the *combination* of ideas. In this case, the total is indeed more than the sum of its parts.

Responds positively to creative presentations: The Presenter likes a presentation that has solid content but is also exciting. They are very receptive to creativity.

Reads group interactions effectively: Other styles, such as the Counselor and the Communicator, will have an intuitive sense of group reactions. The Presenter, however, is more able to *consciously* identify group interactions and to classify those into meaningful patterns. The Presenter combines observational prowess with logical analysis to produce a meaningful explanation of group process.

Wants the information presented to be substantive: Nothing irritates a Presenter more than a presentation that has lots of flash and little substance. They may well regard such presentations as trickery, or as unprofessional behavior.

Often unconsciously measures others' competence: It feels as natural for Presenters to take a measure of others' competence of as it does for more relationship-oriented individuals to check out others' emotional response.

Sees the potential of an idea: The *Thinking-Dreaming* skill combination leads the Presenter into logical exploration of new possibilities. The end result is often the discovery of potential that others may overlook. When you want someone with whom to explore potential strategies, a Presenter may be just the person you are looking for.

Often fills the role of facilitator or mediator: The skills that make them good facilitators and mediators include group observational skills, the ability to interpret and explain group process, and a capacity to generate multiple options.

Is driven by vision: The *Thinking-Dreaming* skill combination allows Presenters to become energized and mobilized by their vision. This sometimes causes them to become more driven and directive than people expect.

Non-Verbal Indicators

The manner in which they present themselves is important to this style, and the non-verbal uniqueness of Presenters relates to this factor. It is what I call the *read and respond phenomenon.* More naturally than any of the other styles, the Presenter will shift into appropriate non-verbal responses. I have chosen some of the most obvious examples to share with you.

The Handshake: Most of the other styles have handshakes they prefer; however, this is not so for the Presenter. Instead, as Presenters approach the person they are about to greet, they quickly (and unconsciously) read how the other party is preparing to greet them. Without thinking about it, they will match the other person's greeting style.

Facial Responses: When in a significant conversation, the Presenter's facial expressions will reflect the message being sent. The face of the Presenter is a mirror of the speaker's comments.

Masking Behavior: While Presenters can register responsive facial expressions as noted above, there are times when they will do just the opposite. That happens when they are in a situation that requires neutrality. This is often the case in a negotiation or crucial discussion at a professional level. At those points, they can assume a neutral facial expression even when they have considerable feeling about the issue being discussed.

Distance for Connection: The Presenter is very aware of appropriate distance, and will make adjustments depending upon signals from the other party about how much space they need to be comfortable in an interaction.

Distance for Boundaries: The Presenter's personal style can lead people to feel they have an invitation to a greater degree of closeness. When the person responds to that signal, Presenters sometime feel a degree of discomfort. In those instances, they will move back almost imperceptibly and send a subtle signal that the interaction is becoming a bit too personal. This works most of the time.

The other group of non-verbal behaviors related to the Presenter style reflects the *Dreaming* skill dominance. Those include:

Upward Gestures: When in discussions, Presenters will often gesture with palms upward.

Inflection: When discussing a new idea, they are likely to use an upward inflection. This is most obvious when the upward inflection occurs at the end of a key sentence.

Shifting: Presenters will often shift about when presenting. This keeps them mentally moving; it means they are not going to become earthbound. This tendency can be detected on the soles of their shoes, because Presenters often create a circle of wear on the ball of the foot.

The Maturity Factor

Even though each style has its unique strengths, it is clear that everyone can misuse behavioral preferences. While competence is a major driver for Presenters, and they will work hard to avoid pitfalls of the "maturity factor," no one is perfect. Some of the following descriptions will likely hit home for Presenters.

Since this is of greater concern to the Presenter than to some of the other styles, let me provide a bit of perspective.

The eight style strengths are best viewed as neutral. Whether we express these style traits as a weakness or strength is to a great degree a function of maturity. When a person has not developed a sense of balance or has not sought to grow personally, he/she is more susceptible to making poor behavioral choices. Rather than considering the misuse of a behavior as an innate weakness in the style, it is more constructive to address it as a function of maturity. Some of the common behavioral areas where the maturity factor is most likely to be evident are noted here.

Ideas without Action: It is only natural for Presenters to love their ideas. However, this can result in the Presenter continuing to explore those ideas long past the time when it is important to move into action. A Presenter who fails to move from exploration to application may lead others to view him/her as being unrealistic or out of touch.

Devaluing the Practical: The temptation to discount the counterpoint skill is another maturity issue. When the Presenter engages in this behavior, it is a two-fold activity; they tend to exaggerate the importance of concepts, while downplaying the value of practical activity.

Wit as a Weapon: Wit and humor are positive interactive attributes of Presenters. If they become defensive and threatened, this asset can quickly turn into a liability. In this case, wit becomes sarcasm – which is not humor at all. Sarcasm can more accurately be described as "crooked anger" which creates a toxic environment that others come to resent.

Intellectual Intolerance: Because they enjoy intellectual exploration, Presenters can become intolerant of those who exhibit less theoretical insight. This can be summed up as the idea, "Think like me, or you're not thinking correctly."

Indiscriminate Learning: The desire to increase their level of expertise can lead Presenters down the path to information overload. They fall into the trap of pursuing learning events with little concern for applicability. When this happens, there is an obvious need to select wisely rather than pursue a knowledge chase that ends in loss of focus.

Dodging Discomfort: People who are constantly calling for more action and quicker results can make Presenters uncomfortable. An immature response to that discomfort is to avoid the person who causes it, but the resulting loss of contact is generally counter-productive.

Never Enough: Having high expectations of self and others is a positive motivator for Presenters. However, when taken to an extreme it results in unrealistically high standards. Others resent this judgmental, blaming attitude, and it is likewise damaging to a Presenter's self-esteem to live under their own dictum of "never enough."

Presenting to the Presenter

While Presenters like creative and constructive ideas, the quality of the presentation will often be a key factor when they judge the value of a proposal. Even a good idea that is poorly presented will be immediately suspect. To receive a positive response, prepare a well-defined and well-conceived presentation that makes use of charts or graphics where appropriate. Their appreciation for creative approaches prompts Presenters to explore options, so feel free to generate them yourself.

This style values positive, pleasant approaches in face-to-face dealings with others. Expect Presenters to show good social skills, and to understand nuances easily.

Non-Verbal Tips

You will find that the Presenter reads your non-verbal communications naturally and reacts to them intuitively. Therefore, it will be important to:

- Avoid exhibiting negative postures such as turning away, refusing eye contact, or not giving a facial response to positive overtures.
- At the other extreme, do not become overly excited in your responsiveness to the point that you begin broadly gesticulating.
- Respect the need for physical distance when the Presenter is conceptualizing.

DO'S AND DON'TS

Do	Don't
• Show excitement in response to new concepts that you may support • Explore alternatives rather than harp on differences • Make proposals to which you would like a response • Be direct, crisp, and factual • Be creative • Demonstrate the potential in your proposals • Use visuals • Allow Presenters time for internal assessment	• Take a blunt, confrontational approach • Attempt to corner the Presenter and nail down a commitment quickly • Lose patience • Be closed to exploration • Be surprised by a Presenter's intense approach at key points • Assume that no verbal response means the Presenter missed your point

SOME WELL KNOWN PRESENTERS:

Woodrow Wilson

Carl Sagan

Barbara Walters

COMMON PROFESSIONS FOR PRESENTERS:

Academic

Marketing Management

Training

Technical

THE PRESENTER

Skill Combinations:

Other-Motivated and *Thinking:* This style is able to engage and connect through the use of social charm – humor, wit, and keen observation.

Thinking and *Dreaming:* Presenters like to be excited by creative, forward-looking ideas; they are also generators of ideas themselves.

Other-Motivated and *Dreaming:* Presenters are open to the potential of other people's ideas.

Chapter 16

INTERPERSONAL TECHNOLOGY

THE SEVENTH STYLE

THE COUNSELOR

The Counselor

A Brief Portrait

A few years ago, the Wonder Works Carpet company began experiencing some significant difficulties keeping people informed and included. In response to the situation, they decided that a position of "Communication Coordinator" would be an important addition to the corporate staff. Once the position was defined, it was very clear that Barry Callaway was a natural for the job. Barry was extremely pleased to be offered the position, and now three years later, is firmly convinced the job was made for him.

Even so, in many ways, Barry made the job what it has become. He has continued to look for ways of reinventing the communication function, so that what started out as a position to address a specific problem is now a vital component in the company. The role has expanded far beyond simply being a central source to coordinate and deliver communications; it is now a leadership position in setting company attitudes and managing company culture.

Today is the third anniversary of his new job, and as Barry thinks back on those three years, there are a number of factors that have led to it being such a successful endeavor. Probably first and foremost was his strong commitment to good communication – to people being informed. Barry can remember how frustrated he was when people were complaining that the company did not care about them.

As he discussed his concern with other managers, it became clear to him that some people were much less concerned about that issue than he was. It was then that Barry began to realize he had a higher degree of sensitivity to such things as morale, inclusion, and employee satisfaction.

In addition to the commitment he feels, Barry is aware of a number of specific skills that have made him effective in this position. One attribute that he has utilized from the beginning is his ability to garner lots of information through informal channels. It is not uncommon for people to stop him and visit in the hallway at work. It first began to dawn on Barry just how vital a tool this was about two weeks after he took the job. He was shopping in a local grocery store when a fellow employee spotted him in the frozen foods aisle and initiated a conversation. Twenty minutes later, more chilled and much, much more informed, Barry was very aware what an important tool informal communication could be in his new job.

People have come to Barry with lots of "way-out" ideas, but his strong practical side has helped him weed out the suggestions that might have threatened the credibility of the program. While he may have missed a few creative initiatives, he is clear that he would rather err on the side of practicality than risk losing credibility while striving for creativity.

For Barry, trust is very important in allowing him to feel the freedom to work effectively. On the disappointing occasions when he discovers that he cannot trust a person, he finds it very hard to move beyond the need for a personal relationship. Even when he knows he must make the adjustment to a more business-like and less personal relationship, Barry finds himself asking why it has to be that way.

There is no doubt that communication at Wonder Works Carpet is viewed in a much broader context than simply written material or internal memos. The broader context includes identifying issues, responding to concerns, and listening respectfully. It means being aware of sending messages through our demeanor as well as our directives. It also means communicating with customers in a manner that reflects the company's desire to serve them well.

A couple of months back, Barry was invited to join a consulting firm that specializes in communication. While he was flattered, he felt a loyalty to the company that has given him the opportunity to develop his skills. More importantly however, his current position enables him to make an impact, which is a tremendous motivator for him. Without a doubt, Barry feels he is right where he belongs.

UNDERSTANDING THE COUNSELOR STYLE

Tracing the Tree

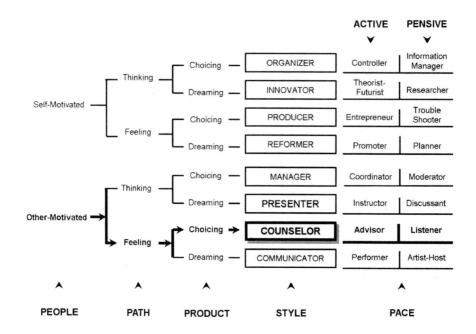

Skill Dominance:

The three major skills that combine to produce the Counselor style are:

Other-Motivated – when engaging in relationships
Feeling – when decision making
Choicing – when implementing tasks

Preferred Pace

The degree of intensity with which the Counselor expresses these three skills will be influenced by the Pace factor: *Active* or *Pensive*.

When Counselors are more *Active* in preferred pace, they will be inclined to enter into relationships more rapidly and to trust more readily. They will also find it difficult to wait for things to happen.

When more *Pensive*, the Counselor will be inclined toward the role of listener. They are more naturally empathetic than any of the other styles.

TEN KEY WORDS

Warm	Humorous
Intuitive	Relational
Entertaining	Big Picture
Responsive	Emotional
Personal	Quick

Major Driver: Positive interaction coupled with practical results

Distinguishing Characteristics of the Counselor Style

Listens with Head and Heart: The Counselor listens from the other person's point of view. It is more natural for the Counselor to practice empathy than for any of the other styles.

A Little Visit would be Nice: Counselors want to build personal relationships as a basis for conducting business. Put another way, they are more comfortable working with an individual they feel they know and can trust.

What a Difference a Difference Makes: This style is motivated by making a positive impact on their environment. Knowing that he or she has *made a difference* to others is a major source of satisfaction.

Don't Fence Me In: Counselors are de-motivated in situations where they are required to work alone for long periods of time. There is a direct connection between human contact and their motivation.

I Still Like You, But: When a conflict is unavoidable, the Counselor will seek to reinforce the relationship before engaging in the conflict. Protecting relationships is very important.

The Need to Complete: Counselors will become restless and impatient when it is obvious that things that need to be done are not *being* done. Relationships are important, but results count.

Let's Settle This Right Now: Their practicality and their relationship skills make Counselors helpful mediators. The Counselor's role as mediator is reinforced by a need to help people resolve differences, and their belief in the fairness of compromise.

It Just Makes Sense: Counselors trust their personal history when making decisions and solving problems. They will intuitively move to the practical solution and be ready to act. They will have less patience with the theoretical or abstract.

Non-Verbal Indicators

Much of the tenor and tone of the way I have described the Counselor centers on the relationship factor. Therefore, it would be surprising if most of their non-verbal behavior were about anything besides relating. Many of the Counselor's non-verbal behaviors are expressions of the desire to make connection, develop trust, or let someone know they care. It may help to explore these behaviors in two categories: response behaviors and expressed behaviors.

<u>Response Behaviors</u>

Head Nods: The Counselor will nod frequently during conversation with another person as a means of making connection.

Smiles: They will smile in response to a smile from another person.

Active Listening: Many of the physical attending behaviors related to active listening are second nature for Counselors. These include: facing the speaker, keeping an open posture, and maintaining appropriate eye contact. All these behaviors encourage the other person to continue talking. They also establish the Counselor as a good listener.

Synchrony: Along with the Communicator, who we will discuss next, the Counselor has the most natural tendency to match the posture and body positions of the person with whom they are interacting.

<u>Expressed Behaviors</u>

Handshakes: The Counselor is a softer version of the Producer. While the Producer's behavior is prompted by the need to make impact, the Counselor's intent is connection. Counselors will extend their hand well into another's personal social space, making positive contact. Still, they will not do so in an invasive or assertive way; their approach has a welcoming sense about it.

Proximity: The Counselor is comfortable standing closer to others than is the general population. Their need for affiliation is higher than their need for personal space. However, they are generally aware if they are creating discomfort in the other party, and will move back to an appropriate distance.

Appropriate Touch: Given the choice, Counselors would prefer a pat on the back, or a brief tap on the shoulder, rather than a formal handshake. Counselors have had to become aware of the new politically correct realities regarding appropriate touch in the workplace.

The Maturity Factor

There are some specific points to be aware of when Counselors exhibit immature behaviors. These center on issues concerning relationships and an unrealistic pragmatism. The specific behaviors most commonly seen are:

Overly Sensitive: Negative comments that focus on the problem at hand, not on the person, are generally considered valid feedback. When behaving immaturely, there is a tendency for Counselors to react to those negative comments in a defensive manner. In these situations, they have difficulty separating an objective comment from a personal attack.

Red Cross Nurse: The tendency to become a rescuer is a consequence of becoming overly invested in other people's situations. This leads to a feeling of resentment when others don't respond with appreciation or seem take their efforts for granted.

The Simple Way: The Counselor's desire to take the practical approach can make it difficult to take the time and effort to consider alternatives. This leads to oversimplification of issues with an immature Counselor. In the work setting, it results in more of a maintenance-type approach rather than a cutting-edge approach.

Warm and Fuzzy: Relationship issues are emphasized over task issues at the expense of getting anything done. In the work setting, this translates into a loss of productivity. In the personal realm, it causes a loss of direction and momentum.

Who Cares: Their strong grasp of the practical makes it difficult for an immature Counselor to tolerate theoretical discussion. This attitude robs them of intellectual breadth.

Hidden Grudges: The less mature Counselor prefers to avoid confrontation. As a result, they may hide resentments and harbor hurt feelings for long periods. Rather than being direct about their anger, they may express it in indirect ways, such as being non-supportive, letting other people down at crucial moments, or failing to pass on critical information.

Relating with the Counselor

Relationship and trust are the basis for interacting with this practical and personable individual. However, while building relationships is important, the drive to find practical solutions to problems also means the Counselor is a pragmatist. The desire for fairness and justice, along with the need to produce results, gives the Counselor an interesting combination of compassion and concealed impatience.

While they are open and receptive, Counselors often make decisions based on their emotional responses. Anticipate a good hearing and a positive and supportive atmosphere when working with this style.

Non-Verbal Tips

The Counselor invites others to build relationships and looks for non-verbal cues of their willingness to do so. To communicate this willingness:

- Respond with synchrony
- Show enthusiasm about feeling statements or feeling issues
- Use soft *Choicing* behaviors such as downward movement and inflections, but couple this behavior with affiliating signals

DO'S and DON'TS

Do	Don't
• Engage in personal conversation • Be willing to make personal revelations • Spend a longer period of time building rapport • Respond positively and reinforce early concessions • Stress fairness • Give plenty of feedback	• Ignore signals of reassurance • Avoid interpersonal issues • Withhold information that can legitimately be shared • Discount issues such as morale or personal concerns • Overemphasize power • Overlook comments from less powerful people

SOME WELL KNOWN COUNSELORS:

Gerald Ford

Mother Theresa

COMMON PROFESSIONS FOR COUNSELORS:

Human Resources

Helping Professions

THE COUNSELOR

Skill Combinations:

Other-Motivated and *Feeling:* This is the most obvious and probably the most dominant skill combination for Counselors. It is the force behind their need for developing personal relationships based on trust. This is the most visible behavior distinctive to the style.

Other-Motivated and *Choicing:* This combination is the basis for the Counselor's remarkable capacity for empathy. Being personally invested in others (*Other-Motivated*), and being practical enough to see the other person's point of view (*Choicing*), encourages empathic responses.

Feeling and *Choicing:* This combination produces a need for practical and reasonable approaches for how things get done. Counselors are quick to see practical solutions and are prone to want to act on them.

Chapter 17

INTERPERSONAL TECHNOLOGY

THE EIGHTH STYLE

THE COMMUNICATOR

The Communicator

A Brief Portrait

Michael Moran is a relatively new member of the Wonder Works Carpet team, having been with the company for less than five years. Michael is the manager of the customer services function. During his tenure, he has instituted a number of innovations that have caught the imagination of key customers and have differentiated the company from the other major brand names in the industry.

Most of the innovations have been a fascinating combination of being responsive to the "people issues," coupled with new technological advances. For example, Michael conceived and implemented the ICR (Instant Customer Response) program. The ICR program involved the development of a sophisticated database that is constantly updated to provide instant answers to key customers. This information allows immediate tracking of customer orders within the plant, and also answers technical, pricing, or marketing questions when the customer requests information. If the system does not have adequate information on a given topic, the program will trip a mechanism that contacts the company representative responsible for that key account. Each major account has a minimum of two representatives who team up to be available around the clock. They make every attempt to provide virtually "instant response" to the customer. The ICR is only one of several inventive initiatives Michael has implemented.

This kind of activity has made Michael quite popular with his fellow managers. They enjoy being identified with projects that are considered cutting edge and result in such positive responses from customers.

A part of what has allowed Michael to hatch one new project after another is his avid curiosity about anything that appears new and different. This has resulted in Michael showing up at some very unlikely places for a manager of customer services. For example, during this past year he attended the major technology event in Las Vegas attended mostly by computer gurus and information managers. His level of interest and very personable manner resulted in several very lively discussions about the application of some of the latest technology.

As a consequence of his obvious visioning ability, Michael has been offered jobs by two start-up companies. While flattered by the offers, Michael is clear that the position he has at Wonder Works Carpet is a better fit for him.

He is confident about their product, and he is very pleased with the response of their customers. Positive responses are a source of great job satisfaction for him.

When Michael was in junior high, he played a major role in a school play and wowed the audience, and he is still able to "steal the show." He has been wise enough to create audiences that can maximize his opportunity for interaction with significant numbers of people.

In his present role, he has created an environment that is not only positive, but encourages people to have fun. Humor is evident in the daily give and take between fellow employees, and spills over into interactions with customers. Michael has helped employees understand that they are not just delivering a product; they are imparting a feeling about the company. This positive experience is what many key customers talk about when they describe their dealings with Wonder Works. There is a program in place to train customer service representatives in how to pass along that "good feeling" that is so important to the company's customer service strategy. The program, dubbed PET (positive emotional transfer), is a foundation of the approach taken at Wonder Works Carpet. Thanks to the inspiration by Michael, it works!

Nowadays, when he comes in with a new proposal that is outside the norm of traditional customer service, Michael gets a ready hearing – and most often an easy approval. He is an accepted and respected member of a very diverse team. This acceptance and respect, along with the success he has experienced with customers, is the reason he says "no" to other offers that come his way. Michael has earned and is enjoying being a valued part of the management team.

UNDERSTANDING THE COMMUNICATOR STYLE

Tracing the Tree

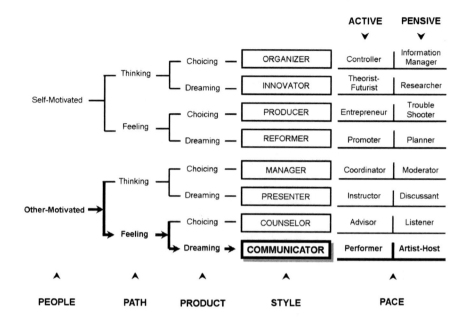

Skill Dominance:

The three major skills that combine to produce the Communicator style are:

> *Other-Motivated:* when engaging in relationships
> *Feeling:* when decision making
> *Dreaming:* when implementing tasks and creating options

Preferred Pace

More *Active* pace Communicators are inclined to be both visual and verbal. They are seen and heard more often. They are usually more comfortable in roles that put them in the presence of others. They will be high-energy and expressive.

The *Pensive* Communicator often chooses other avenues to make contact. Their medium may be music, poetry, writing, or some form of craft.

TEN KEY WORDS

Warm	Humorous
Entertaining	Novelty
Newness	Big Picture
Personal	Quick
Responsive	Relational

Major Driver: Positive "People Response"

Distinguishing Characteristics of the Communicator Style

Use of Personal Energy and Charisma to Create Positive Response: The Communicator will often make contact with others by using humor, cleverness, or general charisma. They are often described as the "life of the party." Being entertaining and exciting are among the Communicator's trusted tools.

Energized by Novel, Creative Concepts: With the exception of receiving a positive response from others, there is little that excites Communicators more than a new, different, and promising idea. They will often become champions of such inspirations, since they quickly recognize the value of ideas.

Reads the Signals: This style focuses on reading group reactions more than individual responses. They can make the intuitive shifts necessary to gain a positive response from the group.

Creative when Brainstorming or Sharing Ideas: Creativity is closely related to significant personal interactions. The more intense the interaction, the more energy generated for the Communicator.

I recently found myself in a group of six Communicators who were assigned the task of coming up with a new marketing program. Their initial anticipation reflected the group's confidence in their ability to produce new and exciting ideas. Their positive anticipation made the air seem to crackle with energy. Each new suggestion was met with an addition or expansion of the original idea. There was also lots of laughter and kidding around, as people reacted to various contributions that were made. The energy, zest, and playfulness of the group provided the stimulation for some terrific new programmatic innovations.

Makes Decisions "Out Loud": Group interaction plays a big part in this style's creation and development of innovative ideas. A similar phenomenon occurs in their decision-making process. Many times, Communicators may come to a meeting not having made a decision about a certain situation. As they discuss the problem at hand, the act of talking about it helps them reach the desired conclusion. In this situation, they suddenly sense that they have the solution to the problem, and will often announce their decision with a great deal of energy and confidence. For those observing this behavior, the seemingly spontaneous decision can be surprising and bewildering.

Likes the Big Picture; Loathes Detail: Most Communicators readily admit their strong preference for the broad overview when addressing a problem. They are almost unanimous in their dislike of managing details or of being assigned repetitive tasks. One Communicator put it this way, "I can think up ideas for hours, but don't ask me to carry out those ideas. That's best left to someone else. I'm a big picture person."

Takes a Left Turn: We are all familiar with Robert Frost's poetic image of the road not taken. Communicators are more comfortable than most with taking the road less traveled. Put another way, this style is more comfortable with the unorthodox than most people. They register a higher degree of acceptance of non-traditional individuals, and are less threatened by new approaches and new concepts. They are more likely to take the "left turn."

Capitalizes on Cooperation: In contrast to those who prefer working alone, the Communicator has the polar opposite response. Having a sense of positive synergy through cooperation enhances their contribution.

Welcomes the Future: Seeing possibility, sensing new trends, and strongly identifying with these concepts comes naturally for Communicators. While others are struggling to adjust, they are often using the new language, adopting the new styles, or enjoying the excitement connected with the new movement. Since Communicators are very people-oriented, they are often strong advocates for new causes that they see as having social or humane consequences. Hollywood and its many Communicator style entertainers are visible examples of those who take up new causes with flair and enthusiasm.

A Little Fun: Of all the styles, Communicators more commonly mix work and play. This is not to suggest that they are unproductive, only that they discover ingenious ways to make work fun. They often bring humor to situations that would otherwise be overly serious.

Non-Verbal Indicators

A constellation of non-verbal behaviors exhibited by Communicators can be described as *high-contact* behaviors. These behaviors produce positive responses and build relationships. Communicators enjoy meaningful contact more than most people, even if they are only going to relate with the person for a brief time. For that reason, the behaviors described below are routinely exhibited by Communicators with both frequency and consistency.

Bright Smiles: The Communicator's smiles are not your half-hearted, weak-sister smiles. They are broad, appealing, Julia Roberts kind of smiles that capture the attention of those around them.

Vigorous Assent: It would be a misleading understatement to describe the Communicator's response during conversation as a "head nod." They display an intensity and an energy that implies real involvement. This will be true even when the person is part of an audience listening to a speaker. They often catch the attention of the speaker, and may have them speaking just to them.

Gestures, Gestures: Communicators' gestures are frequent, broad, and dramatic. They are more inclined to "talk with their hands" than any of the other styles.

Spontaneous Responses: The Communicator may respond with a kind of enthusiasm and energy that is a surprise to others.

Color: The Communicator's clothing is often more colorful than the other styles. At times, their dress can appear almost costume like.

Buoyant Walk: Communicators walk more on the balls of the feet, which gives an impression of moving energy when they walk.

The Maturity Factor

In each of the prior seven styles, we have explored their strengths but have also provided a word of caution about the points of vulnerability. As with the other styles, the Communicator's most common points of vulnerability are usually the result of a misuse or overuse of the style's strengths due to a lack of maturity.

Intensity Rules Reason: Communicators' skill combinations produce a degree of intensity that, if not managed with some level of maturity, results in life choices that simply are not reasonable. Our media is filled with stories about Communicator style entertainers making ill-founded choices.

Impulsive Commitment: Operating from a strong emotional context can lead to commitments that are made too quickly.

Ignoring Details: Most Communicators will readily tell you that they hate dealing with details. Without the discipline of maturity, they may choose to ignore details even when those details are critically important.

Misjudging Character: The Communicator sees potential in people, and is excited by that potential. Unfortunately, individuals do not always live up to our vision of their potential. Without consistent reality checks, Communicators can maintain their unrealistically high expectations. When this happens to Communicators, they are extremely disappointed in the other person, and sometimes feel betrayed.

Overly Dramatic: Communicators naturally have a flair for the dramatic, but immaturity can lead to *overly* dramatic behavior. This can result in others tuning them out, or to their reactions being discounted when things are indeed dramatic.

Form over Substance: The immature Communicator runs the risk of responding to presentations that are dramatic and exciting without checking the facts. This makes them susceptible to accepting misinformation.

Mood Swings: Communicators experience things more intensely than most of the other styles, but immature Communicators do not handle this intensity well. They are more likely to be candidates for mood swings.

Burn Out: A more common result of Communicators' high-energy, high-impact lifestyle is that they may ignore warning signals and continue to push until the point of exhaustion. The outcome is what we call burnout.

Interacting with the Communicator

This style greatly prefers positive interactions, and will make active efforts to have a constructive interchange. On the other hand, if they perceive that an exchange may be unpleasant, they may have a strong negative emotional response. In seeking the best climate for interacting, it will be important to provide as much factual *and* emotional information as possible. Knowing how others feel is very important to the Communicator. This style enjoys an interaction sprinkled with humor, creativity, and new approaches.

Non-Verbal Tips

Communicators enjoy building constructive relationships based on affective response. Therefore, a high degree of synchrony and animation are key non-verbal behaviors.

DO'S and DON'TS

Do	Don't
• Build positive, personal relationships • Show excitement about ideas you can support • Spend time relating personal accounts and anecdotes • Provide "big picture" proposals • Be patient with the process of expanding options prior to decision making • Exhibit energy and responsiveness • Listen to feelings	• Cut off a Communicator's sharing because it is not directly task oriented • Bog down proposals with too much detail • Make light of creative but seemingly unworkable proposals • Be too serious • Confront harshly • Ignore subtle signals for compromise

SOME WELL KNOWN COMMUNICATORS:

Ronald Reagan

Bill Cosby

Larry King

Princess Diana

COMMON PROFESSIONS FOR COMMUNICATORS:

Entertainment

Persuasion/Sales

Helping Professions

The Arts

THE COMMUNICATOR

Skill Combinations:

Other-Motivated and *Feeling:* This combination of skills prompts the Communicator to seek to forge relationships with others. This style enjoys interacting even when the relationship will be brief or short term. They often surprise others with the level of emotional intensity they express even when it is obvious that the opportunity to relate will be brief.

Other-Motivated and *Dreaming:* Communicators often see possibilities in individuals that other styles may overlook. This tends to make them more accepting of other people than are the other styles. It also means they may find themselves feeling disappointed when others do not live up to the vision they have of them.

Feeling and *Dreaming:* The more intuitive, global, thinking process (*Feeling*), coupled with the preference for creativity (*Dreaming*), creates a tendency to generate broad-brush concepts that are fresh and unusual.

Chapter 18

THE CONTEXT OF COMMUNICATION

Now that you are equipped with the added insight *Interpersonal Technology* provides about the influence of style, you can apply that knowledge to create positive interactive strategies. Let me begin with a simple statement: *The basic tool for achieving positive interaction is communication.*

When referring to communication, I mean both the overt and the non-verbal. It might be more accurate to describe these as the visible and the invisible. Most people acknowledge the existence of non-verbal signals, but remain unaware of their impact in daily interactions.

A helpful analogy in our high tech world is to think of this invisible world as being like our wireless environment. When there is a positive field around us, we can tune in and engage in internet activity. However, if the field is not present, we can produce and send as many messages as we wish, but nothing happens.

Similarly, it is important to remember that to achieve effective interactions requires us to create a climate where constructive interchange can take place. If, for example, I sense another person has no respect for my values or for me as a person, it will be difficult for me to engage in meaningful conversation.

I should also point out that *effective* interaction does not always mean positive, agreeing conversation. It may occur even where hard issues are raised and clear differences are sharply expressed. The point is that a correct strategy enhances the likelihood of constructive and productive conversation.

A second premise is that creating the positive climate described above, coupled with the correct approach at the concrete or visible level, is the basis for positive communication strategy. This means recognizing *significant style differences* and being willing to make the appropriate adjustments. The following four situations are provided to allow you to explore the use of *Interpersonal Technology* as a strategy tool.

FROM STYLE TO STRATEGY

Your knowledge of style gives you the means to generate immediate strategies to create more productive interactions. The following conversations demonstrate the ways in which many interactions go awry, and offer some positive solutions.

While it will be apparent how opposite skill sets can create these natural interpersonal challenges, it will be equally apparent that with some conscious strategy, far more positive results are also possible. You may even see a bit of yourself in one of these interactions, which will make it particularly meaningful.

Communication Challenges

Styles: *Organizer* and *Communicator*

The Organizer and the Communicator have different dominant skills that influence their interaction patterns. Those differing skills are reflected in the chart below.

	ORGANIZER ⬇	COMMUNICATOR ⬇
PEOPLE	Self-Motivated	Other-Motivated
PATH	Thinking	Feeling
PRODUCT	Choicing	Dreaming
PACE	Active *or* Pensive	Active *or* Pensive

Due to their differing skill combinations, a conversation between these two styles could go something like this:

Communicator: "I'm glad I caught you in your office. I know that you have a trip to take today, but I really wanted to visit with you before you got away." (Upbeat and positive)

Organizer: "Well, you caught me." (Noncommittal)

Communicator: "You know that I have been concerned about the fact that our customer service employees have not had any training in a long time, and I think it is causing us some difficulty with our customer relations. I have found a program I think will be really helpful."

Organizer: "Where did you find the information?"

Communicator: "I visited with the head of customer service for Z-Line Corporation. The training has really been a hit with them."

Organizer: (Silence)

Communicator: (Continuing, with hesitation) "Since you have the people working for you that serve our wholesale customers, I wanted to discuss it with you as soon as I could. I think we should sponsor this for both wholesale and retail customer service employees."

Organizer: "What makes you think this will work for our people?"

Communicator: "Why are you being so negative about this? Your department has received as many complaints as ours. We need to do something about this." (With emotion)

Organizer: "Just calm down. I didn't say we didn't need to do something about it. I'm just not sure you've checked this thoroughly enough."

Communicator: "I feel really comfortable with this program. I visited with the Z-line manager for almost an hour, and I got my concerns met."

Organizer: "I hope this is not as expensive as the last program you recommended. If we had done that program, it would have destroyed my budget."

Communicator: "I told you I have looked into this. The cost is reasonable. I think we should go ahead with it."

Organizer: (Silence; direct stare)

Communicator: (Voice rising) "If you are not interested, I will go ahead with my own department."

Organizer: "Have you got any literature on the program?"

Communicator: "I can get some literature, but I want to be able to start this initiative before you get back in ten days."

Organizer: "I will not commit to this until I have seen some information and received some other references."

Communicator: "I think it may be best for me just to go ahead on my own, and you can see the results in our improved performance."

Organizer: (Silence)

Communicator: "Have a good trip." (Without enthusiasm)

Organizer: "Thanks." (Neutral)

Dynamics:

This vignette demonstrates some of the common misunderstandings that can occur between Communicators and Organizers.

In the initial interchange, the enthusiasm expressed by the *Feeling-Dreaming* Communicator is met by the neutral response of the *Self-Motivated* and *Thinking* Organizer. This difference created an atmosphere where the individuals were on a different wavelength from the beginning.

The *Other-Motivated* and *Feeling* skills dominant in the Communicator prompt this style to share personal experience, and to use that experience as the basis for decisions. The *Thinking-Choicing* skills of the Organizer result in a need for data and specific information. This difference can lead the Communicator to assume that the Organizer does not care, or does not value his/her experience. Conversely, it may cause the Organizer to view the Communicator as being less thorough than is desirable.

To Communicators, the Organizer's silence often feels judgmental, or is taken as a signal of disagreement. This may cause the Communicator either to withdraw or to become intimidated.

When there is a difference of opinion and Communicators feel the need to express their point of view with greater feeling, Organizers tend to see this as being unduly emotional, or they may become uncomfortable and withdraw.

Negative assumptions based on not recognizing and appreciating skill differences can create significant misunderstandings. The challenge is to recognize and adjust appropriately when interacting with other styles.

Strategies for the Communicator:

What are the strategies (actions, attitudes, behaviors) that the Communicator could employ that would make him/her more effective when interacting with the Organizer?

A Communicator who is aware of the Organizer's style preferences would know at the outset that the Organizer is not inclined to be relational and expressive. Knowing not to expect that kind of reinforcement, and choosing to operate from a more independent stance would make a great deal of difference in the feelings generated.

Second, being aware of the Organizer's need for concrete information, the Communicator would do well to assemble some written material. Expecting the Organizer to respond to an enthusiastic recommendation in lieu of hard data is not a well thought out approach.

Third, in terms of timing, to insist on an immediate decision without sufficient time for analysis is invite a "no" from the independent-minded Organizer. Allowing time for the Organizer to come to his/her own logical conclusion would be an important strategy to apply in this situation.

Strategies for the Organizer:

What are the strategies (actions, attitudes, behaviors) that the Organizer could employ that would make him/her more effective when communicating with the Communicator?

First, an Organizer who recognizes the Communicator's need for a greater degree of relational interaction could decide to move beyond his or her comfort zone and engage in a brief social conversation.

Second, validating the more intuitive approach by acknowledging that the program probably has merit would help lessen the Communicator's defensiveness. The Organizer could then remind the Communicator of his/her need for objective information.

Third, Communicators need a response when interacting. It would have been helpful for the Organizer to indicate a time when the Communicator could expect a response, likely resulting in a more positive outcome.

Conclusion:

It can make significant differences in our interchanges to consciously take into account what we know about the other person's style, and be willing to accommodate some of their obvious needs.

Communication Challenges

Styles: *Counselor* and *Innovator*

The Counselor and Innovator have opposing skills:

COUNSELOR ↓		INNOVATOR ↓
PEOPLE	Other-Motivated	Self-Motivated
PATH	Feeling	Thinking
PRODUCT	Choicing	Dreaming
PACE	Active *or* Pensive	Active *or* Pensive

A typical interchange that demonstrates the particular challenges when Counselor and Innovator styles communicate may sound something like this:

Counselor: "I came by to talk with you about the program we are to present in two weeks. Is this a good time to visit?"

Innovator: "It's fine."

Counselor: "How have things been with you? I haven't seen you at the last couple of planning meetings."

Innovator: "I have been busy, and the meetings didn't seem all that important."

Counselor: "Have you enjoyed the new project you have been working on? I would really like to hear more about it."

Innovator: "Well, I'm just getting started on it. So far, I'm in the research phase, so I don't have an opinion about it just yet."

Counselor: "Maybe we could get together over lunch next week and you could share with me how it's going. I'm interested."

Innovator: "I'm not sure just how far along I will be by then, but it's nice of you to ask."

Counselor: "At any rate, maybe we can talk today about reporting on the project we have just completed. The program date will be here before we know it."

Innovator: "What is the date for that presentation?"

Counselor: "It's the twenty-eighth, just two weeks from today. It seems important that we agree on who will cover what portions of the report."

Innovator: "I have the written document ready to turn in, which substantiates my point of view. Why don't you make a verbal summary?"

Counselor: "But we were asked to make a joint report, and I think that means both of us are expected to participate in the presentation. Do you have a problem about our doing this together?"

Innovator: "No, I just need to consider how this can be done. I haven't given it any consideration until now. I think it is more than dividing up the material. There needs to be a concept, an approach that is challenging."

Counselor: "Maybe so, but this is not rocket science we're reporting on. It seems to me we need to agree on a plan of action and move forward."

Innovator: "Give me a couple of days to think about it, and let's get back together."

Dynamics:

This interchange has not been as productive as either party would prefer. It is even likely that both went away holding some unspoken opinions and feelings that were more negative than is apparent from the dialogue alone.

Both styles are influenced by their dominant skills, which show up in subtle ways in the conversation. For instance, the Counselor's skill in *Other-Motivation* makes him or her want to develop personal relationships. Every attempt to do that was thwarted by the Innovator, whose *Self-Motivated* and *Thinking* skill combination creates a desire for more privacy. In this case, one individual seeks intimacy, while the other prefers reserve and a more formal relationship.

Secondly, the Innovator's dominant skills in *Thinking* and *Dreaming* encourage development of concepts, with less regard for schedules and practical concerns. This behavior leads the Counselor to assume that the Innovator is being impractical and unrealistic. In contrast, the Counselor's more pragmatic and spontaneous behavior seems rash and overly simplistic to the Innovator.

Over time, such silent judgments can affect the quality of a working relationship between these two styles. It requires special awareness by both parties to avoid the negative consequences that can occur.

Strategies for the Counselor:

What strategy should the Counselor employ to be most effective in this situation?

Once it became obvious that the Innovator had prepared a report to present alone, it is very important that the Counselor move from inviting collaboration to confronting, taking a more independent stance. By doing so, the Counselor will be on a common communication level with the Innovator. The following are possible responses for the Counselor:

- ✓ Acknowledge the withdrawal behavior that suggests an unwillingness to work together, and invite the Innovator to respond.
- ✓ State that unless the Innovator is willing to join in a cooperative effort, the Counselor will be presenting independently.

✓ State that the action the Counselor will take is to prepare a parallel paper and report to the manager that he/she was not able to gain cooperation for a common report.

Strategies for the Innovator:

What strategies could the Innovator take that would improve the situation?

It is not uncommon for Innovators to believe in the superiority of their ideas. This can result in a reluctance to share ideas until they receive credit for them, and one way of guarding their ideas is withdrawal. In this case, an obvious strategy would be to recognize this tendency in themselves and to choose a more open behavior.

This choice would move the Innovator outside their normal comfort zone, which would clearly improve the interchange.

Communication Challenges

<u>Styles</u>: *Presenter* and *Producer*

The dominant skill profiles for the Presenter and Producer are:

	PRESENTER ↓	**PRODUCER** ↓
PEOPLE	Other-Motivated	Self-Motivated
PATH	Thinking	Feeling
PRODUCT	Dreaming	Choicing
PACE	Active *or* Pensive	Active *or* Pensive

Considering the difference in dominant skills, a conversation that could easily occur between the Producer and the Presenter might play out something like this:

Presenter: "I understand that you have talked to Francis (their mutual boss) about initiating a sales blitz for our software product."

Producer: "Yeah, she liked the idea; I told her we need to get started right away."

Presenter: "Since I serve as co-team leader on the project, I would like to have been consulted about this approach, and I would have appreciated being brought in on the meeting with Francis."

Producer: "I would have invited you, but you were out of town yesterday, and once I had the idea, it just didn't seem like a good idea to wait.

Presenter: "Well, even so, I…." (Interrupted)

Producer: "It doesn't matter because she gave the go ahead to move forward on the project. So it all turned out OK." (Moving in closer and closer to the Presenter's space.)

Presenter: (Backing away slightly) "I have two concerns: first, we need to have a united front for our two departments and my not being in the meeting seems to send a different message. It sets a precedent I would rather not have set."

Producer: "I think you're being overly-sensitive about this. I just wanted to get us underway, and every day is critical in our launching the new product."

Presenter: "I know you see it that way, but it is a concern for me. And that suggests another issue. We will need to talk about timing for this sales initiative."

Producer: "I think we should set up a strike force team, and be prepared to present to our sixty key clients in two weeks." (Expressed loudly and enthusiastically)

Presenter: (Obvious concern in voice) "You know that we have not completed all the documentation that will make the product as reliable and useful to the customer as it needs to be. We still need to work on how we are going to ensure the best use of the system for our customers!"

Producer: "Yeah, I know that, but if we wait for your tech-types to perfect everything, we'll miss our window of opportunity. Just give them a deadline of ten days, and it will get done."

Presenter: "It's not that simple…." (Interrupted)

Producer: "It *is* that simple. Just get your group hopping and we can both be winners!"

Dynamics:

It would be all too easy for both parties to walk away from this encounter making negative assessments of the other. From the viewpoint of the Producer, whose *Feeling-Choicing* skills encourage the person to act on a decision as promptly as possible, the Presenter will be seen as far too hesitant.

The Presenter, dominant in *Thinking-Dreaming*, will want to look at potential problems and answer them through the documentation process. The Presenter will be prone to look upon the drive for action as overly simplistic and shortsighted.

The *Self-Motivated* skill of the Producer may allow him/her to misinterpret the interpersonal concerns expressed by the Presenter. Thus, the Producer may see the Presenter as overly sensitive, or too concerned about "people issues."

The Presenter, predictably, may experience the Producer as being insensitive or unconcerned about relationship issues. The non-verbal exchange may leave similar differences of perception, with the Producer seeing the Presenter as lacking in power, and the Presenter perceiving the Producer as overbearing or overly aggressive.

Strategies for the Presenter:

What can the Presenter do to improve this interaction?

In order not to appear lacking in leadership initiative, the Presenter will need to call on the *Dreaming* skill to make a case for an alternate approach. Noting positive outcomes will be much more effective than a negative approach. Pointing out the negative consequences, though valid, may lead to being labeled indecisive. Being positive can earn the Presenter a place as peer. A focus on positive outcomes might be:

- ✓ Having sufficient time could allow us to package the product in a manner that would truly represent a new generation in health care.
- ✓ Testing the product can give us greater opportunities for explaining how this application will work.

✓ Training the sales force will make a significantly improved first impression.

Strategies for the Producer:

What can the Producer do to improve this interaction?

The Producer's preference for *Self-Motivated* behavior can lead to discounting more relational *Other-Motivated* behavior. Therefore, engaging in more *Other-Motivated* behavior could improve the interaction. Some suggestions are:

✓ Stop interrupting
✓ Stop labeling: "You are just...."
✓ Start listening

When discussing getting something done, it is a matter of pragmatism versus possibility. The Producer wants to seize the opportunity and make something happen. The Presenter wants to explore the possibilities and look for improvement. Thus, a second strategy for Producers is to be willing to consider possibilities before insisting on action. In this case:

✓ Start exploring ideas with the Presenter

Communication Challenges

Styles: *Manager* and *Reformer*

These two styles have distinctly different dominant skill sets, as indicated in the following chart:

	MANAGER ↓	**REFORMER** ↓
PEOPLE	Other-Motivated	Self-Motivated
PATH	Thinking	Feeling
PRODUCT	Choicing	Dreaming
PACE	Active *or* Pensive	Active *or* Pensive

Having different dominant skills affects the manner in which each style communicates. Style also creates assumptions and expectations that play a big part in our interactions. The conversation below is an example of the challenges that occur when a Reformer and Manager interact.

Reformer: "I'm glad you're in your office; I have this terrific concept that I think can revolutionize our organization."

Manager: "That sounds pretty dramatic. Are you sure 'revolutionize' is the right word?"

Reformer: "Revolutionize is an understatement. If we are visionary enough to move beyond the rest of the pack, we can be in a class of our own … way beyond everyone else!"

Manager: (Remaining calm) "Just what is this revolutionary new concept?"

Reformer: "You don't sound very excited about hearing it. Can't you show a little enthusiasm and creativity just once?" (Mildly irritated)

Manager: (Continuing to appear calm) "It's just that I have to implement the programs we commit to, and I don't want another situation like the last one where my group was working eighteen hours a day to meet the impossible deadline we had."

Reformer: "You just don't like challenges. Come on; listen to this idea. I think we can turn a corner well ahead of anyone else in our industry."

Manager: (Cautiously) "OK, let's hear it."

Reformer: "I think we should combine our over-the-counter health care products with an identifiable health care maintenance system."

Manager: "We're not in the health care maintenance business; we're in the health care products business." (Voice rising indicating concern.) "I can't believe you are suggesting this!"

Reformer: (Undaunted) "We can be the first brand name provider of health care products <u>and</u> services. I think it will increase our sales as well as put us in a totally new revenue stream."

Manager: "Do you have any idea how much effort it would take to develop the kind of alliance of health care professionals we would need? Not to say anything about the number of HMO's who buy our products who would suddenly see us as competition."

Reformer: "Sure it would take some effort, but I have already talked to some people in medical recruitment, and they assure me it's do-able."

Manager: (Sarcastic) "I'm sure they do, but for a hefty fee."

Reformer: (Becoming more energized) "Look at the potential. Cost is not the issue here. We could make an impact on the direction of our industry for years to come."

Manager: "Who else have you discussed this with, before coming to me?"

Reformer: "Just one person from the trade press, who thought it was a tremendous concept."

Manager: "WHAT? You've already leaked this story?"

Reformer: "Nah, he's a friend who promised me there would be no story until we're ready. I just wanted to test the waters."

Manager: "We're going to have to have to call a meeting with our boss; I am very concerned about this putting us at risk in more ways than I care to think about." (Moving away from the table and preparing to leave)

Dynamics:

It is obvious that with his/her *Feeling-Dreaming* skills, the Reformer is excited by creative and inventive ideas. It feels natural to generate exciting and innovative approaches to personal or business challenges. Their *Self-Motivated* and *Feeling* skill combination also makes Reformers comfortable with boldness. Risk feels less threatening.

In contrast, the Manager's *Thinking-Choicing* skill combination encourages prudence and a common sense approach. In addition, the *Other-Motivated* skill prompts the Manager to consider the impact of new ideas on people.

As a result, these two styles are likely to feel conflict at several points:

- The Reformer may perceive the Manager's prudence as a lack of commitment, or as a being an obstacle to progress.
- The Manager will likely feel frustration due to the belief that he or she has to monitor the "wild" ideas of the Reformer.
- The Reformer seeks to gain commitment by sharing excitement; the Manager seeks to create equilibrium by remaining calm. Their desired outcomes are often very different, and both can misunderstand the other's motivation.
- The Reformer is concerned with concepts and possibilities, while the Manager is concerned with consequences and present challenges.
- The Reformer may discount the Manager by seeing him/her as unimaginative, while the Manager may discount the Reformer by seeing the person as unrealistic and dangerous.

Strategies for the Manager:

What actions could the Manager take that would improve the interaction?

The Manager's tendency is to be the guardian of current policies and procedures, while the Reformer is a change agent. Therefore, when the Reformer makes bold proposals it is difficult for the Manager to refrain from objecting and defending the current situation. Some things the Manager can do differently are:

✓ Allow the Reformer to go through his/her presentation without interrupting with objections. Listen and ask clarification questions. Do not commit; just get the information.
✓ Ask for a time out. Gain time to allow a reasoned response, and to give the Reformer a chance to get a bit of emotional distance from the proposal.
✓ Work not to appear as a constant blocker and negative influence. Agree where possible; differ without being combative.

Strategies for the Reformer:

What actions could the Reformer take that would improve the interaction?

✓ Recognize that prudence has its place, and demonstrate appreciation for the Manager's contributions.
✓ Slow down your Dreaming and listen to the implementation (*Choicing*) issues the Manager is raising.
✓ Put the brakes on your high-speed approach as a safeguard against being so far out in front of the Manager and others that no one is in the same place as you.

Chapter 19

Applying *Interpersonal Technology* in Our Life and Work

You have been given detailed and specific information for strategies on how to be more effective in relating to each of the eight styles. What you will find in the next few pages are 10 overarching principles that are invaluable guides for making the best use of the system.

Ten Major Guidelines

The cliché, "information is power," is only true if you make use of the information. In that sense, the proof of the pudding for *Interpersonal Technology* is having you, the reader, put it to good use. I have provided information at the end of each chapter that can serve as to resource when you want to review strategies for dealing with a particular style. However, there are some broader guidelines that provide the basis for the strategic use of *IT*. These are provided with the intent of encouraging and guiding you to reap the maximum benefit from the *Interpersonal Technology* system.

Guideline One: *Understand the value of speaking "style language."*

If you have traveled outside your country to a destination where a different language is spoken, you know how much you appreciate it when someone speaks to you in your native tongue. Even if the person's use of the language is less than perfect, we appreciate the effort.

In many ways, it is the same issue with style language. Each of us has a way of interacting that is based on our worldview – our style. And that style is based on our inherited and acquired preferences. We are most comfortable when people seem to sense our preferences and "speak our language."

In that sense, making the conscious decision to broaden our range of reactions and responses to include the style preferences of others is the first step in learning to speak style language. The opposite reaction is to say, "I am just who I am, and people will have to take me like I am." If you say so, that will be the case, but remember others don't always have to like it!

One valuable feature of *Information Technology* is that you don't have to change your personality in order to make use of the system. Instead, you learn how to alter your reactions and responses at crucial points to fit the worldview of someone with whom you want to have a positive interaction.

The first step in learning to become fluent in style language is deciding to make use of the insights that style information provides, and to stretch our range of behaviors to include another person's perspective. If you do that effectively, you will discover their appreciation that you have chosen to speak to them in their native tongue.

So, Guideline One reminds us that making the decision to develop our skill in becoming multilingual is a necessary first step.

Guideline Two: *Communication is verbal and non-verbal, and we need to make use of both.*

We read and hear how important non-verbal behavior is in our overall communication processes. For the most part however, after acknowledging that fact, we largely ignore non-verbal interactions and allow them to operate at an unconscious level. While none of us can stay aware of non-verbal behavior at a conscious level all the time, we can make more mindful use of this component of our interactions at crucial points.

I have provided a great deal of systematic information to help you read non-verbal behaviors. Raising your level of awareness and making use of the insights provided is an essential ingredient your best use of style language.

In order to become better at this process, set aside brief periods to observe the non-verbal behavior going on around you. Over the years, I have sharpened my observational skill by watching people's non-verbal behavior while waiting for my plane to arrive. Another interesting tool is to watch television programs with the sound muted. It will help you discover how much we let words get in the way of our truly noticing subtle signals that give us so much important information.

While I have chosen to emphasize non-verbal body language, I am not suggesting that the words we use are unimportant. They are vitally important, as some of these guidelines will demonstrate. However, the point where nearly everyone can grow the most noticeably is in learning more about the powerful, silent, non-verbal language that is expressed in all our interactions.

Guideline Three: *Remember, only a slight shift in the direction of the other person's style is all that is needed to create a more positive interaction.*

None of us wants to give up our identity to achieve better interactions, and that is not what I am suggesting. Over the years, we have discovered that a slight shift in the direction of the other person's preferred behaviors, both verbally and non-verbally, can have a tremendously positive impact on interactions.

When people make exaggerated adjustments in their behavior to make the language shift we are suggesting, it generally comes across as clumsy and intrusive, and has the opposite of the desired effect. So, when making style shifts, the hint is, "easy does it."

Guideline Four: *Recognize and respond to relationship issues.*

A fundamental factor in our interactions with others is the recognition that people have a preference for how they interact with us. They have a desire to be either more independent or more relational, and they want us to recognize and respond that to that preference. This does not mean that we need to give up our own style of relating. It does mean, however, that we can connect with this person more effectively by making an adjustment in the direction of their preferred behavior.

For example, if we are relating with a more *Other-Motivated*, relational person, using "we" language in place of the more independent "I" language can make a subtle difference.

A very important reminder relates to non-verbal responses. Beware of the conventional suggestion that you need only to mirror the body language of the person to make connection. You will recall that mirroring is effective with the relational person, but may evoke the opposite reaction from a highly independent person.

The rule is, "read before reacting."

Guideline Five: *Recognize and respect the different ways people gather and process information in order to make decisions and solve problems.*

This is partially achieved by supplying the optimum environment for processing information by style preference. For example:

- For Organizers and Innovators, allow sufficient "alone time" for independent thought.
- For Producers and Reformers, provide a high energy, exciting environment.
- For Managers and Presenters, offer opportunities for conversation that can lead to conclusions.
- For Counselors and Communicators, provide opportunities for sharing and encountering that result in new insights.

On an individual basis, pay attention to the times when restricted movement on your part will be important (as is the case with analytical people), and when it is important to be energetic (as it is with more intuitive people).

Guideline Six: *Be aware of how best to interact when people are producing results – that is, when implementing or creating.*

The first step is to remain aware of the two major ways we produce results. Those two ways are the *concrete* and the *conceptual.* Both produce a result – one tangible and one intangible. Respecting both of these work-products can help us respond with greater breadth when dealing with others.

As a point of reference, the Organizer, the Producer, the Manager, and the Counselor are more inclined to produce concrete and tangible results. The Innovator, Reformer, Presenter, and Communicator are more likely to produce conceptual and intangible results.

To help broaden your responses, pay attention to your own preferences so you can make certain to allow room for your less preferred activity.

Guideline Seven: *Recognize that Pace sets the tone and tenor of our personal and organizational environment.*

The way we express our natural pace will affect those who live and work around us. Likewise, awareness of others' natural cadence and how we adjust to it is an important part of making style adjustments.

For example, if we have a high *Active* cadence and we insist that those around us keep up with our "go, go," hurry-up means of operating, we may create a stressful and unproductive environment for others. The same mismatch can occur if we prefer to be laid-back and reflective when others want a more active and energetic environment.

Recognizing and being willing to adjust our pace when necessary is a part of speaking the other person's style language.

Guideline Eight: *Being able to speak style language is a dynamic process.*

It should be obvious by now that an essential element in this process involves our ability to engage in observation, recognition, and behavioral adjustment. That said, people are not static beings. Once we have noticed, identified, and responded appropriately, it does not mean the process is finished. As people shift into differing modes of behavior we have to continue to engage in the dynamic process of appropriate response.

In this sense, we need to keep in mind that speaking style language is a fluid, ever-changing process.

Guideline Nine: *Remember that we do not move people to our comfort zone by exaggerating our behavior.*

Let me explain this guideline with a specific example. Imagine a person who is analytical and logical interacting with someone who is extremely spontaneous and emotional. Now, recognize that the analytical person is very uncomfortable with the other party's strong expression of feeling. Oftentimes in these situations, the analytical person thinks that if they just become more and more restrained, the other person will get the hint and calm down.

In reality, what usually happens is that as the other person senses greater restraint, they instead try harder to connect by *raising* their level of expression.

Remember, you do not enhance interchanges by increasing your own comfort zone (style preference), but by being willing to enter into the other person's comfort zone.

Guideline Ten: *You do not have to change your personality; just know when to make strategic behavioral adjustments.*

An important phrase to remember is "situationally appropriate behavior." It is a reminder that in the *Interpersonal Technology* system, you have the capacity to expand your behavioral choices to meet the needs of another person or situation. Moreover, you can do so with the awareness of the behavioral choices you make and why you make them. Rather than diminish you by asking you to change who you are, *IT* provides you an opportunity to expand your world and broaden your perspective.

I hope that you will sense a new degree of freedom to become truly multilingual.

CPSIA information can be obtained at www.ICGtesting.com
Printed in the USA
238034LV00001B/3/P